THE ALIGNMENT STRATEGY

Copyright

First Printing: 2021

ISBN 978-1-7771537-0-0

Lori Brant

Ontario, Canada

www.LoriBrant.com

THE HAPPINESS COACH

The Alignment Strategy

LORI BRANT

Contents

Introduction

After years of working on my own limiting beliefs and returning inward to align with my natural state of happiness, I began to see that my clients were seeking that too.

As a life coach, clients came to me to help them achieve their goals and when we dove deeply into the motivation behind why they wanted what they wanted, it was often revealed that it was not the goal itself that they actually desired, it was a feeling. Whether it was conscious or unconscious, they believed that once they achieved their goal, they would be happy.

My clients seemed to be so busy doing, going, achieving, working, challenging, or acquiring things that they lost sight of why they were doing what they were doing and ended up drifting from one task to the next, living life on autopilot, numb, oblivious and disengaged. I started to see that only helping clients to achieve a tangible goal did not deal with the original cause of their discontent.

I began asking the same questions during coaching sessions that I had asked myself, like, "What limiting beliefs or outdated strategies were keeping them from their natural state of peace, calm, and happiness? What fuelled their perception that happiness no longer existed within, but was something that needed to be obtained outside of themselves?"

Similar to an apple believing its seeds existed beyond its outer skin, how could I help my clients draw their awareness inward to help them recognize that the seeds of happiness that they were seeking, already existed within them?

This book was written to help people recalibrate how they move through the world by systematically drawing them back inward, to reconnect and align with their true selves. By doing so, their natural state of being can become the foundation for all of their experiences and movement forward.

I have found that by intentionally moving into the Alignment Zone, I am able to create a foundation of creativity, possibility, expansion, and growth for my future plans and actions. Action taken from an aligned state is free from limitation and negative thought and helps me to be attentive, open, and receptive to divine insight and inner wisdom too.

Living from the Alignment Zone has changed my life. Outside circumstances seldom rock my world or throw me into the depths of negativity like they once did. Instead, life has become a gentle rocking back and forth like a free flowing, sea bed plant, undisturbed and untouched by surface storms.

Chapter 1

WHAT ARE WE LOOKING FOR?

Happiness and Alignment

Do you look around at all that you have and still feel like something is missing? Do you want something different but don't know what it is or how to get it? Do you long to feel happy?

What if you could wake up energized for the day, playful and content? What if you could spend an entire day alone, feeling connected and supported like the room was full of loving friends? What if you could find the missing piece that keeps you from the life that you crave?

Have you ever had that experience where you walk into the kitchen and suddenly realize you forgot why you went in there? That is how a lot of us seem to be living our lives. We are just going places, doing things, achieving things. And when we get there, when we get to that place, complete a project, or achieve a goal, it's not long before we think, "Huh. That's not it."

So, what are we looking for? If you are like my clients and me, we had this inkling that something more significant existed beyond our routine lives that was more gratifying than any other experience we had already had. Yet, we could not name it, describe it, or define it. We could only discern the feeling that it would bestow. We would be happy.

However, I believe that the search for something greater outside of ourselves, the deliverer of happiness, was the very thing that was keeping it at bay. The greatness seducing us was our true selves calling us inwardly home. It was who we really were, beckoning our return to live life from our natural state of peace, calm, and happiness.

We have become a society driven by outside experiences, relationships, and acquisitions because our Awareness has drifted away from our natural state of peace, love, and happiness. By drawing our Awareness away from the outside world and focusing it inward, we can connect with who we really are and eliminate our desire to seek fulfillment through external circumstances.

When we were born, we had the natural ability to recognize the magnificence that surrounded us. When we came into the world, it was like a surprise party over and over again. Everything was a bonus to an already fantastic existence. We were supported, abundantly provided for, everlastingly loved because we did not yet have an experience that would make us believe otherwise. We were organically engaged with reality, free, fearless, naturally enthralled moment to moment, and able to appreciate the magnificence within and around us. Just watch the excitement of a baby playing with their toes, their enjoyment at seeing themselves in a mirror, or pure joy that surfaces with a fart. They can naturally enjoy each experience free of concern or judgment.

Our ability to enjoy our experiences and be engaged freely, fearlessly and enthralled moment to moment is our birthright. It is what we were created to do. It is who we are. That ability or state of being still exists and will linger and swell with the simplest of invitations. It is not something to be obtained, acquired, or something to be wrestled to the ground but instead is the access point where the outer and inner are no longer separate. It is where freedom and creativity infuse the human condition and where a sense of peace, calm, and happiness permeate our perceptions and it exists within all of us. We can reconnect with it in the Alignment Zone.

The Alignment Zone is a state of Awareness where we can detach from the body's physical and mental conditions and observe freely and clearly our experience as a physical being interacting with reality. In the Alignment Zone, we can detach from perceived limitations, choose how we wish to respond, and recognize the magnificence that exists within and around all of us.

Living life from the Alignment Zone is like opening the dams of greatness and allowing it to flood your physical form with Universal love. When you're all filled up like that, you don't need anything different than what is. You don't require anything to change either. That means all of your attention can tune into the present moment.

If your attention is not drawn outward to get something, do something, achieve something, then you can be completely present with what's going on. You can interact with the world without an agenda, need, or fear. You're able to observe and appreciate what's happening, clearly, from the internal perspective of Universal Love.

Alignment determines how we respond and interact with the world around us. Here are some indicators that you are in the Alignment Zone.

> **Your mind is calm.** You're not thinking about the future or the past. Thoughts might arise about the future or the past, but they pass through without your mind attaching to them. They don't trigger negative emotions or dictate your behavior in the moment.

Your body is relaxed. All parts of the body are comfortable and calm, and you have a regular heartbeat.

You're open to the suggestions and opinions of others. When people make suggestions or criticize your choices or actions, you hear them and recognize the possibility that their comments could be helpful. You're open to considering them, either then or later, and know implicitly that the decision of whether or not to act on them is free from obligation.

You're open to new experiences. If you had a plan and circumstances change, you can quickly pivot. You know that the change is for you and that there are now gifts that previously would not have been available. When you feel drawn to do something different, there is no fear, resistance, or stressful thoughts about the future. You feel free.

You see the gifts in the moment. Your mind is on the same page as your heart and searches for examples of how the present moment serves you and the world around you. You can consider how you might be growing and expanding even though it might not yet be apparent. You just know the gifts are there, always. You automatically look for a person's positive qualities.

You are self-aware. You can observe your thinking, emotions rising, and the behaviors you are engaging in. You can identify negative and positive changes within your mind and body and bring Awareness to the circumstances to find evidence of triggers and limiting beliefs.

When something that appears negative happens, you don't react. You may have the initial thought that what is happening should not be happening, but you quickly seek and acknowledge the gifts in the moment. You can embody the complete knowing that what is happening should be happening, and your mind begins seeking evidence of how that is so.

You are drawn easily towards your next action. You simply move into effortless and smooth action. Your mind is focused, time seems to pass quickly, and your body feels as refreshed as it was before the action was taken or even more so. There is no hesitation.

You recognize how you are always supported. Your mind will consider all the ways it is supported in the moment. Even if it is just the chair you are sitting on or the air you are breathing. You can recognize that the Universe is continuously supporting you, showing up as friends, family, objects, and circumstances.

You recognize you have everything you need. There is no need to seek anything other than what is provided in the moment to feel peaceful, calm, and happy. You have the inner knowing that you have everything within you to feel connected with your natural state.

You love and appreciate others, just as they are. People don't need to change for you to be happy and you understand that those around you do not dictate your inner peace, calm, and happiness. You know that they are the perfect version of themselves, showing up as themselves. You also understand that how they perceive your interaction with them is their business, and how you perceive your interaction with them is your business.

You love and appreciate all of yourself. In this moment, you are perfect just the way you are. Even if you are crying and yelling, you can recognize that that must be what should be happening, because it is. You can observe your behavior and love yourself completely. In Alignment, any negative thought, emotion, or action is observed and viewed as an opportunity to transform a limiting belief that would have otherwise gone undetected. The mind recognizes the beauty and perfection in your body and your experiences.

How would your life be different if you knew without a shadow of a doubt that you were always supported, abundantly provided for, and could organically engage with reality, freely, fearlessly, enthralled moment to moment?

How would that feel? How would your life be different if you were feeling all full and satisfied? How might your day be changed if you embodied that freedom, that power, that inner joy? How might you react to a long line at the grocery store or stop and go traffic? How might you respond to your credit card bill or someone who is angry with you?

Guess what? That fullness and freedom exist within and around you. That's your natural state. Greatness, universal love, is who you are. You do not have to achieve, acquire, develop, learn, purchase anything outside of yourself to experience any of that fullness. It is just waiting to be unleashed and experienced by you.

Are you ready to acknowledge all of you? Are you ready to see, feel, and live in your greatness? Are you ready to question your fears, stay present in the moment, stand in your power, laugh often, and let love ooze out of you? Are you willing to do what it takes, break old habits, get off autopilot, and clear out what keeps you from unleashing your greatness and living life from the Alignment Zone? If so, say, "Yes!"

I thought I was living in the Alignment Zone when I was happy.

I remember the time when I was dressed in a long, slim, white wedding dress, with a glass of champagne in my right hand and a microphone in the other, looking out at the sea of people that loved and supported me. I felt tears hover as I suddenly realized in that moment, I was happy. I was finally happy. I had arrived. I was there. I did it.

I had transcended the loss of my father, survived witnessing the ravages of my mother's cancer, and traversed a debilitating diagnosis. At 25 years old, I realized that I did it. I had made it through the challenges, and I would be OK. I was married, someone loved me, my heart was full, and I was finally happy.

That was until the underwear was on the floor. The pair that someone left for me to pick up because they were too lazy to do it themselves. It's not like I didn't have enough to do. If someone would just pick up their damn underwear, then.... I'd be happy.

Just when I thought I had nailed it, finally did what I had to do, got where I needed to go, achieved what I needed to achieve, something would happen outside of me, as insignificant as someone leaving their underwear on the floor, that would result in the joy, that peace, just slipping away, leaving that familiar hollowness, begging to be filled.

Time and time again, I found myself focusing on the outside, trying to control what was happening or determine what people needed to do or be like so that I could be happy, but each time, I was disappointed. Whatever happiness I found, it eventually would dissipate and I'd go searching for something else to fill the gap.

Somewhere deep within, though, I was sure that an unwavering state of peace and calm existed. It silently called to me, beckoning me home. I yearned for its fullness, to feel satisfied and content, yet, it eluded me at every junction.

If I was ever going to tap into my natural state of peace, calm, and happiness, I needed to do something different.

When it became clear that focusing on the outside was not working, and the old way of doing things was no longer acceptable, I decided that I would stop looking to outside circumstances, people, experiences, and things to trigger happiness inside me. Instead, I decided to work as fiercely on my inward goal of happiness as I had worked on my outward goals of the past.

To do that, I needed to be very clear about what my definition of happiness was.

I was surprised to find that it was not a state of extraordinary pleasure or orgasmic experiences. Instead, my definition of happiness encompassed experiences consumed with calm, peace, neutrality, subtle joy, and satisfaction. It was that type of happiness I wanted to underpin my life and be the foundation of my perceptions.

Imagine having a pure, unobstructed moment, void of influences from the past and limiting expectations for the future. Imagine having a profound meditative experience, completely awake, eyes wide open while physically, mentally, and emotionally engaged in what is happening in the moment. Imagine a wave of love washing over you and recognizing that this is how life is meant to be observed, felt, and tasted.

Now, what if that experience created a profound wave of gratitude that enveloped you, swirled in and around your entire being while you remained physically, mentally, and emotionally engaged, eyes wide open, completely awake, and aware?

In that state, you would see others for who they truly are, without their stories or their problems because in that moment, you were being YOU, without your story, without your problems, your limitations, or your fear.

Now imagine that this fantastic, uncontrollable series of experiences triggered your heart to swell and expand so that you were filled with unconditional love.

Amazing, right?

When I found that I could experience life like that in the Alignment Zone, I chose being in the Alignment Zone to be my highest priority, the goal that superseded all other goals and made it my full-time job. Not just during meditation or when I was writing in my journal the five things I was grateful for, but all day, every day. It would become the goal to end all other goals.

Is that something you'd like to experience?

Your life may be calling you, drawing you inward, to move you past what keeps you separated from what is possible. One way to experience all of who you are is to work on the limiting belief patterns and fearful projections of your future.

The Alignment Strategy can help you to free yourself from the layers of thought that block those waves of gratitude, swirls of joy, and unconditional love from your experience.

Are you open to living life differently? Are you ready to make Alignment your number one goal?

Chapter 2

THE ALIGNMENT ZONE

Alignment

Different words can be used interchangeably to name or describe alignment. I believe that it's the actual naming of it that makes it elusive because to label it makes it seem like a thing. Alignment is not a thing, something to be achieved or acquired. Alignment is a state of being that is uniquely perceived and experienced individually. For the sake of this book, I will attempt to name and describe alignment.

Alignment is where we can detach from the body's physical and mental conditions and clearly observe our experience as a physical being interacting with reality. The Alignment Zone is where the mind and heart are in sync with one another. It's where our limiting beliefs have no power to create discomfort or draw us away from the true essence of who we are.

I have found that alignment is something I experience moment to moment as a state of Awareness focused inward, where I can perceive the world clearly without distraction and without being obstructed by negative limiting beliefs or perceptions. It means that I can perceive whatever I perceive as a neutral observer, open to infinite perceptions, possibilities, and interpretations. I can just enjoy the moment. I can witness what I'm feeling, listen deeply, hear what is being shared, and observe the whole of the experience without judging or comparing it. When I am in the Alignment Zone, I believe I am whole and complete just as I am and I can observe that wholeness and completeness being reflected back from the world around me. I have also found that my state of being in the Alignment Zone is changeable and fluid. Some people have described it as that loving sensation that washes over you in deep states of gratitude or love. Others have described it as formless or bodiless. This, my friend, is who you are, who we all are.

Think of a time when you were so engrossed in a pleasurable activity that time was lost. Think of an instance when you were looking into your child's eyes, astonished by their existence and swallowed up by their perfection. Think of a time when you were showered with love for no reason by someone special. These types of experiences can give you a glimpse into your natural state of being. Notice how there are no over-the-top, emotionally ecstatic type experiences, but instead, experiences that wash over you emotionally, like a gentle, loving breeze wrapping itself around you.

I first became aware of The Alignment Zone during a meditation. For a few minutes, I felt the lightness of being empty, and at the same time, the expansiveness of feeling absolutely full beyond the confines of my body.

That, to me, was my first glance at who I really was. After that experience, living unintentionally became unacceptable. I wanted more of whatever happened during that meditation because those minutes of freedom were more satisfying than anything I had ever experienced before.

I had discovered that my limiting beliefs were the only thing standing between me and living life from that aligned state experienced in the Alignment Zone.

What are limiting beliefs and where do they come from?

A limiting belief is a thought with negative emotion(s) attached to it that we believe to be true. Belief patterns form when we interpret what we experience and file it away in our memory like files in a filing cabinet. As we decode more and more experiences, our mind creates files by bunching similar experiences together, finding generalities and commonalities amongst them. These files make up our subconscious or unconscious mind, a culmination of general ways to respond to similar situations and become the foundation of our perceptions. Some are helpful and some create stress and limit our perspective.

It was my understanding for a long time that I chose my beliefs and behaviors by carefully evaluating available evidence, using previous experiences and intellectual reasoning. What I discovered was that I absorbed a lot of beliefs without realizing it and they operated undetected. My mind protected them by intentionally negating any evidence that opposed them.

LES Loop

After years of working on my own limiting beliefs and working with clients on theirs, I began to see patterns. These patterns often led to a link between an early childhood incident and the strategies that were developed to deal with it. Childhood incidents were not always traumatic events. More often than not, the earliest childhood memory of the limiting belief/

emotion/strategy pattern resulted from a single, non-threatening event. For instance, a playground pick, the burying of a rock, or a sweet Grandma who always said yes.

I found that if I could isolate the pattern and find the connection to where it originated, I could profoundly shift the client forward. By bringing Awareness to how, where, and why the pattern was created, how the pattern influenced their present-day experience, and helping clients open up to new perceptual possibilities, they became free from the limitations that had previously permeated their whole life.

Limiting Belief - Emotion - Strategy

The LES Loop is a looping pattern of thought, emotion, and behavior that keeps an individual out of alignment and creates the perception that their experience is LESs than what it actually is. The patterned Loop creates the illusion that you need something outside of yourself to be happy, peaceful, and calm.

A LES Pattern Loop comprises a **Limiting Belief, Negative Emotions, and Negative Behavioral Strategies**. Let's take a look at each.

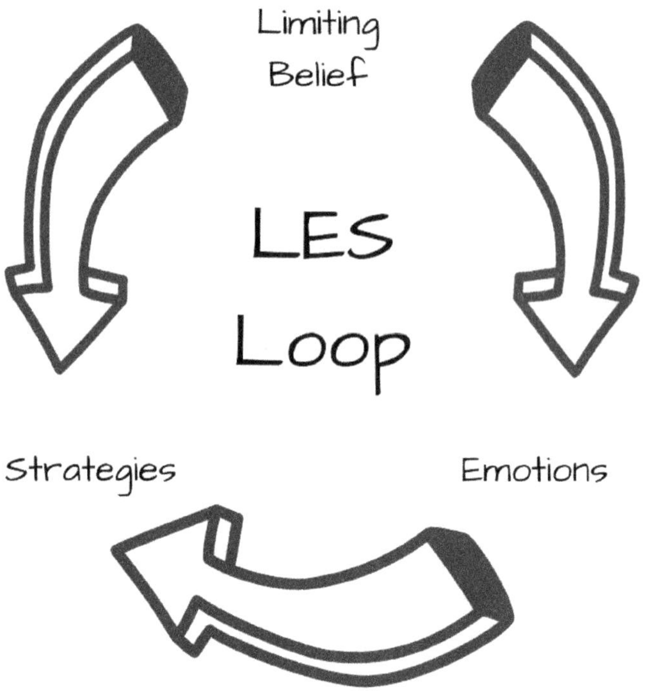

A limiting belief is a thought that limits the information our mind uses to create our perception in the moment and obstructs our ability to recognize who and what we really are. That separation between what the mind is thinking and the true essence of who we are results in emotional and physical discomfort. A limiting belief can be as simple as the thought, "I am weak. I am not enough. I am too much. I need to be in control. I need to be safe. I'm unmotivated. I need help. You are mean. You are controlling me. I can't focus. You're distracted. The world is crazy. You're crazy. You need to change." The mind creates the illusion that we need more than we have or need to be more than what we already are. That illusion creates discomfort because it goes against our true nature.

When we experience emotions like sadness, anger, frustration, or agitation, that experience lets us know that we have a limiting belief that has been triggered within us and we are moving out of alignment. Any form of discomfort is our internal alarm bell indicating that we are out of alignment.

A negative behavioral strategy is a behavior that we believe will reduce or eliminate the negative emotions or physical discomfort created by the limiting belief. However, the strategy often triggers other limiting beliefs and negative emotions rather than reduce or eliminate them.

As children, we had little experience or knowledge about how to deal with negative thoughts and emotions, so we often created strategic patterned responses based on what we knew at the time to keep ourselves from having to feel discomfort in the future. The problem with these old strategies is that they were designed by a child with a child's mindset, and they may no longer be an appropriate or helpful adult response.

During a coaching session, one or more of the three, a **L**imiting Belief, **E**motion, or **S**trategy, will stand out as something I need to explore more deeply with the client. I have found that if I can identify one of the three, I can usually help the client connect to a LES loop that may be influencing their present-day experience. Take my experience of a playground pick, for example.

My anticipation and excitement could hardly be contained as us kids assembled in the open space, bordered by the Benner family on the left, the Moffats to the right, and the parking lot fence to the local McDonalds where over billions of people were served.

A few of the older kids held wooden bats swinging at the air, anxious to get started and some held leather ball gloves with the pocket worked in ready to catch a pop fly. Standing there with tar bubble-stained feet, I proudly beat my fist into the center of my new, flat, shiny vinyl glove.

The two oldest kids made themselves captains, and each took turns as they began to select their teams. As the youngest and only girl in the neighborhood, I waited anxiously, yearning to be chosen quickly as, one by one, the pool of players dwindled. This childhood ritual continued until there was only one kid left unchosen. Me.

Each team captain offered me up to the other, saying, “You can have her.”

“No, you take her.”

Embarrassment and shame rose within me like the sucked-up drippings in a turkey baster. I’m not good enough, I’m not wanted, I’m not desirable, I’m not valued, I’m not worthy. Devastated and rejected, I quickly turned, jumped the ditch, and bolted home to hide my childish tears.

My younger self began making connections between my beliefs about what not being picked said about me and the feelings that engulfed me. “Nobody wants me. I'm not good enough. I'm not valued. I never want to feel ashamed or embarrassed like that ever again."

In that moment, I began to unconsciously develop elaborate strategies to become the best, to be the one doing the choosing, to be the first one chosen, to ensure I would never be chosen last again. As those limiting beliefs and emotions became cemented in my mind, I began to engage in a string of strategies to live by to control my reality and keep myself from feeling the embarrassment and shame I experienced that summer day on Merritt Pkwy. I created a Loop.

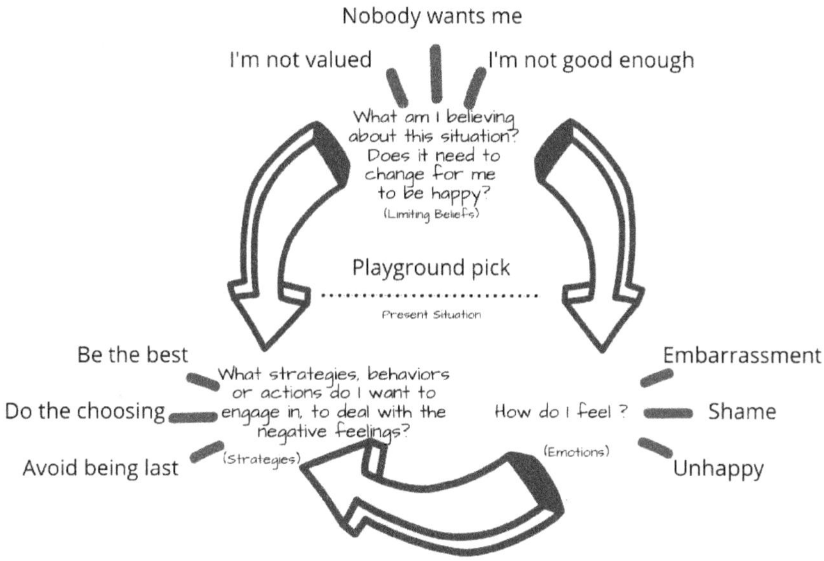

My strategy to be the best steered me to join a baseball league and later become the pitcher. That way, I could play the whole game, be more valuable to the team and be in a position where I would never get cut. My strategies reinforced my belief that the better I am at everything I do, the greater the possibility I'll never be last, rejected, or excluded again.

It didn't stop on the baseball field. I strived to be the best student, best athlete, best teacher, best mother. I sought opportunities to stand out, be popular, get along, make other people happy. When there was a risk of being embarrassed, ashamed, not good enough, devastated, rejected, or last, I dodged it.

In Grade 10 Physical Education class, the teacher made us do sit-ups for one minute as a requirement for the Canada

Fitness Test, and I couldn't do a single sit-up. I didn't realize it, but the Muscular Dystrophy was settling in, preventing me from being able to do them. I masked my embarrassment with laughter and the teacher yelled at me for fooling around. Within days, I dropped the course.

My action to quit gym class in grade 10 was directed by the limiting beliefs and the strategies created by the playground pick I had experienced years earlier. My strategy was to avoid all instances where I might be last.

The negative impact of the strategies on my life was most apparent when I could no longer carry them out due to the MD. When I could no longer be the best, I no longer had an effective strategy to deal with all those emotions I felt on the field that day, and those same emotions were all surfacing again in my adult life. I was paralyzed by not knowing what to do, how to handle my feelings, or what actions to take, which led me into a deep depression. Having MD was challenging. However, my depression was a result of an old Loop that got triggered and old strategies that were no longer working. By learning how to eliminate the Loop, I stopped the uprising of old, outdated beliefs and strategies that no longer served me, I was able to get out of the depression and deal clearly and effectively with my present-day experience of having the MD.

That process brought me to this work and my understanding of how to live life differently in the Alignment Zone.

The Alignment Zone

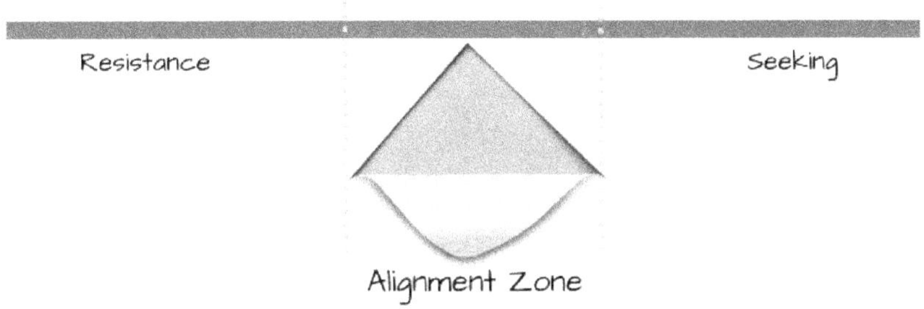

Notice the area in the diagram between the two dotted lines. That is where I aim to stay during my day. In the Alignment Zone, I can observe my experience without attaching to any LES Loops (limiting beliefs, emotions, or strategies), connected to them, and instead, can perceive my experience from the natural state of peace, calm, and pleasure that already exists within and around me. I am aligned with my true self.

Suppose I get pulled out of alignment by attaching to a limiting belief, resisting what is happening in the moment, or by seeking something more than what I already have. In that case, I can choose to draw my Awareness inward, back into the Alignment Zone. It becomes a gentle, flowing dance. When I find myself too far out from the center, I can change direction and simply glide back inward.

When I say moving in or out of alignment, there is actually no moving. The true essence of who you are, who I am, is everywhere. It's inescapable. We can't physically move toward or away from it because it is always present. It is our Awareness that shifts.

I use the word "move," to describe what the experience is like, not to indicate what is actually happening. To move away from the Alignment Zone is like reading an eye chart in the optometrist's office. The big letters are super clear, but as you make your way down to the bottom row, the letters are more difficult to see. The letters are still there, they are just hard to make out.

The more you resist or seek something different from what you already have, the blurrier "who you really are," becomes. The more triggered LES Loops you have, the more difficult it is to perceive reality clearly from the true essence of who you are. Reality becomes blurred.

I believe people expect that there is a state of enlightenment where they will forever live in the center of the Alignment Zone and will no longer be drawn outward by the temptations of the mind or outside circumstances. I have not had that experience. Instead, I have observed that I tend to move in and out continuously during my day. By becoming more and more aware or present throughout my day, the effort and time required to maintain or draw myself back into the Alignment Zone becomes less and less. **The process of observing my state of being, recognizing when I am aligned, and moving back in when I am not, is what I call the Alignment Strategy.**

That happened one day when I went swimming. I was using the railing, inching my way to the ramp to enter the public pool and I noticed that the tile underneath my left foot was exceptionally slippery. In that moment, I observed my attention shift from being inwardly focused to being outwardly focused. I went from noticing the water's temperature, the cold air on my skin, the smoothness of the rail, the echo of voices in the pool to focusing my attention on my mind's thoughts. I began to project what might happen. I imagined slipping and falling. I imagined breaking a bone and the aftermath of dealing with that. I projected not being able to swim anymore. I observed that my legs felt weak and were shaking slightly. I noticed my heart beginning to race, my body tense, and fear begin to rise within me. The slippery ground triggered my LES Loops.

That all happened in an instant. My negative stream of thought and physical sensations of discomfort, fear, and weakness were letting me know that I was moving out of the Alignment Zone towards resistance. By tuning into the signs that my Awareness had shifted and understanding that my LES Loops were triggered, I could draw my Awareness back in, wait for peace and calm to embrace me, and then consider my options from a state of clarity and openness. I was enlightened, then not enlightened, and then enlightened again. I was in the Alignment Zone, moved out, and then moved back in. I, as Awareness, was dancing with my mind. I used the Alignment Strategy to move back inward and realign my mind with my heart, and perceive my experience wholly, completely, and clearly, just as it was. In an aligned state, I was open to my next, best step forward, and that was not to take a step at all. Instead, I calmly asked for a water wheelchair so that I could lower myself down into it. That seemed like the most loving thing to do in the moment, and doing what is most loving in the moment for myself and others is what living in the Alignment Zone is all about.

Taking loving action or responding lovingly to ourselves and others is in alignment with our true nature. Living life from that state of being is what is most natural for us, and when we're not doing that, it creates discomfort.

The Outside Zone

One time, I was standing at the kitchen sink preparing my lunch and turned to grab the lettuce from the refrigerator. It was a regular, everyday activity, and I did not think about the turning, or my feet, or the floor. That was until my knees buckled. The next thing I knew, I was sprawled on the ceramic tile, staring up at the ceiling, scanning my body for injury.

Huh, I didn't see that coming.

Before that fall, I had spent most of my life living in resistance. Every time something happened outside of me, if I was touched by loss, it would rock my world and shake me to the core. Rolling waves of emotion and negative thoughts would crash into my experience, and the only way I knew how to deal with it was to try to contain it and push it down into the deep recesses of my being where all the things I didn't want to deal with lived. I resisted it all.

Each time a challenge touched me, the lid on those contained thoughts and emotions cracked open and drew me deeper and deeper into a state of resistance, tainting my perception of what was going on in the present moment. My mind was triggering multiple LES Loops with a similar strategy of pushing away my feelings.

Something like a fall, like the one I had in the kitchen, would have broken that container wide open and a flurry of fear, sadness, and desperation would have coated my entire experience. I'd start imagining worse case scenarios, with thoughts like "no one will find me for years and I'll waste away from starvation, mummified on my kitchen floor." Each negative thought overwhelmed me, so my strategy was to shove all those negative emotions back down inside.

That strategy seemed practical because when I pushed my emotions down, it stopped me from having to feel them, and I'd get some relief from the pain. I mistakenly believed that "relief from pain" was equal to or, the same as, peace and calm.

I have come to see that the peace and calm experienced in the Alignment Zone are different than the perceived peace and calm experienced from a sudden decrease in pain, fear, threats, chaos, or change. Many people may unknowingly be living life in a constant state of stress and believing that it's the same as the aligned state experienced in the Alignment Zone. Especially those who have experienced trauma or difficult challenges in life. Their everyday stress levels are so high that any decrease in stress, however small, feels like peace and calm. Relief from extreme discomfort is not the same as being in alignment and loving what is.

I was working with a client and we were trying to identify a time in their life when they felt and experienced their natural state.

"I know, I remember a time when I was aligned," she replied. "When I was walking on a wooded trail as a teenager, I tripped and slipped off the edge. I grasped onto some branches growing out of the side of the hill and began screaming and begging for someone to help me. Finally, after what seemed like forever, an older couple stopped, reached down, grabbed my hands, and pulled me to safety. I was so grateful. I felt peace and calm then." She lived her entire life in a state of stress where her LES Loops were always active and was unaware that there was any other emotional state available to her, except for the temporary state of relief she felt being saved from death off the side of a cliff.

I was unaware, too. When I pushed down those emotions and got relief, it felt good temporarily, but I was still in a state of resistance. It felt better than it felt previously when the emotions were triggered, but the relief was a decrease in stress, not peace and calm. That decrease in stress is a false state of alignment found beyond the Alignment Zone, in the Outside zone.

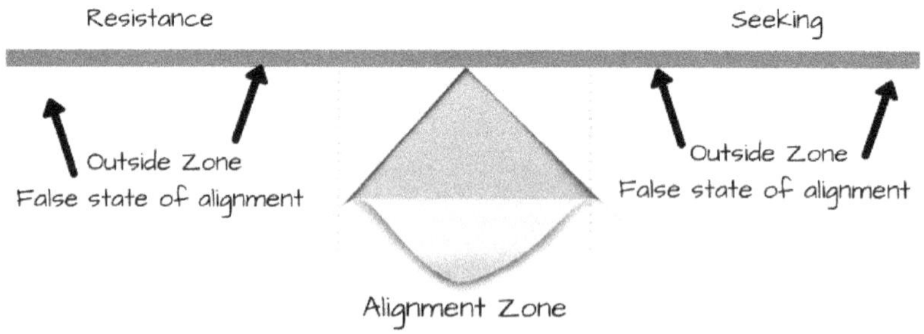

The Outside zone is an imaginary state created by the mind to preserve the mind's perception of the world. It is the culmination of beliefs, emotions, experiences, and predetermined actions used to protect its existence and maintain the illusion of separateness from our true selves. It is where reality is perceived through the mind's automatic activation of old LES Loops.

Do you have emotions that you resist? Have you ever pushed down and ignored negative emotions?

When I was lying on the kitchen floor after my fall, I noticed my initial reaction of tears, sadness, discomfort, and I noticed the thought arise that I needed to push myself through this and get back up again. I thought that if I just walked through my fear, handled this challenge, and stood back up again, I would be aligned. The fall had triggered a LES Loop.

I have learned that the lessening of emotional, mental, or physical pain is not alignment. Those buried emotions prior to pushing through a challenge or loss are still there, inside, affecting my perceptions and experiences.

Alignment is a state of being where the mind is quiet and tuned into the person we are talking to or the experience we are having. It's an acute Awareness of the reactions we're experiencing and the emotions rising within. It's a state of BEing where we are not reflecting on the past or projecting into the future. It's a state where our attention is focused on what is right in front of us, observing, listening, tuned in, turned on, and tapped into reality, just as it is. It's not reactionary.

Being in alignment with who we really are is the sweetest, kindest, most freeing, and loving thing we can do for ourselves and everyone else. Living life from the Alignment Zone keeps us open to infinite possibilities, alternative movements forward, and the gifts in each moment. When we are in alignment, we can hold a space for the people in our lives to be who they are, absent of our judgments or expectations. It allows us to see through our own limiting beliefs, the limiting beliefs of others and helps to create a loving space for their magnificence to be reflected back to them. The greatest gift we can give the world is to live life from the Alignment Zone and move back into alignment as soon as we catch ourselves moving out of it so that the true essence of who we really are can shine.

That's it. Aligning your mind with your heart in the Alignment Zone allows you to live in harmony with the Universe.

I want to help you to intimately understand, experience, and utilize the Alignment Strategy so that you will be able to recognize the difference between living life from the Outside Zone and living life from Alignment Zone. In this book, you'll learn how The Alignment Strategy gives you the choice and tools to move back into alignment whenever you want to feel more peace, calm, and happiness.

The Comfort Zone

The mind tries to convince us that the comfort zone (Outside Zone) is more desirable than alignment.

Imagine sheep escaping through the pen's open door. The priority of the herder would be to close the door to keep the sheep contained. The herder's immediate thoughts might be, "How can I stop this? This is bad. What went wrong? How can we stop this from happening again?"

The comfort zone is like a sheep pen. The mind creates the comfort zone to keep you corralled and controlled and justifies it by making you believe it is keeping you safe. You go along with it because there seems to be reasonable evidence to support that belief. Life appears safer in the pen. So even if you taste a bit of excitement about breaking out of the comfort zone, it's easy to convince yourself to retreat back in because it is familiar, safe, and requires less effort. It's easier for the mind to keep you doing what you've always done because, according to your mind, it takes less work. It's easier to keep LES loops looping than to be consciously aware.

The comfort zone is your sheep pen, and the mind is the herder.

The Mind

It is part of the human condition to perceive, feel, and experience reality through our physical body, specifically our brain. The brain takes in data from the outside and uses that data to create a reality for us. It finds patterns in the data and filters out any information that it has perceived as unnecessary, so processing the enormous amount of data is easier and more efficient.

Therefore, everything in reality is being filtered and judged by the brain. As a result, the brain is not using all the available data in the present moment to create perceptions. According to our brain, entertaining infinite possibilities and considering alternate perceptions that are available in the present moment is not efficient. It takes too much time and energy to sift through it all, and it is much easier for our mind to combine similar experiences, responses, interpretations, perceptions into groups.

The brain categorizes the information like files in a filing cabinet for easy reference and to predict outcomes. Our brain operates with the underlying assumption that keeping life predictable and habitual is preferred and optimal for your survival. In the Outside zone, our brain interprets the information it takes in and creates a perception based on previous experiences. It creates Loops of action based on perception.

This process is beneficial when our brain's patterns and instructions help us maintain alignment with our natural state of peace and calm. But, it's not helpful when data filtering closes us off to information or opportunities and draws us out of alignment.

The mind has a job. It creates Loops to help us remember to look both ways before crossing the street, wear warm clothes in winter, or tie our shoes after putting them on. It allows us to do many things without being consciously aware of each step along the way, and we get to live life on autopilot for routine, essential life tasks. It's a blessing to go through the day taking care of tasks like brushing our teeth, dressing, or driving without having to be aware of every action in every moment and can instead have the mind register the data automatically and carry out the necessary behaviors on autopilot. This really is an amazing gift. I love that I don't have to think about the intricate details of driving or walking.

I had a taste of what it was like to think about every step when I used a mobility walker in 2012 due to muscular dystrophy. Back then, I had to concentrate on every step, carefully inspecting my environment for the unexpected, like loose gravel, an icy sidewalk, or a crack where I'd catch my foot. With each step, my mind was consumed with every movement leaving me exhausted and unable to be present with the people in my life. I truly recognized the gift of the mind's ability to be on autopilot. All this attention to the details of walking prevented me from tuning into the beauty and possibilities that life had to offer.

When the mind tunes into our head's thoughts or conversations, it prevents us from tuning into the beauty and possibilities being offered in the moment and draws us out of alignment. The mind separates itself from the heart and systematically processes our limiting beliefs, emotions, and behaviors of the past. It regurgitates the same old beliefs and behaviors by triggering LES Loops and keeps us confined to our limited perceptions or interpretations of our life. We begin to overlook the beauty in ourselves and our relationships, the intentions behind our actions, and the beliefs that are fueling them. How we interact with life becomes automated.

The Outside Zone's automation may seem peaceful and calm, but that peace and calm are not the same as the state of being experienced when in alignment. I can clean my house and remain in the Alignment Zone, open to the gifts in the moment, present with the tasks at hand, recognizing the smells, and observing my movements. I can be tuned into the sound of the vacuum while my automatic leg movements go unregistered. I am in complete alignment with what I am doing. My mind and heart are on the same page.

In the Outside Zone, my body would be vacuuming and my mind would be thinking about something completely different. Not only are my movements automated, but my mind and feelings are automated too. That's why there is discomfort. Living in the Outside Zone is living with the separation of mind and heart or the separation from the true essence of who you are.

How the Mind Can Lead to Suffering

If the mind is left alone to work separately from the heart, it can accumulate new beliefs and emotional and behavioral connections that don't serve us. In addition to carrying out the basic behaviors necessary to navigate the world, the mind can begin triggering LES Loops and create a make-believe world of past and future.

"Tie your shoes after they are on your feet," the mind might say, and in turn, the body may reach down, put on the shoes and tie the laces without much fanfare. However, if allowed, that simple, neutral, helpful thought can quickly become a raging lunatic on autopilot.

"Those are ugly shoes. I need new shoes. My feet are too big. It's hard to find shoes to fit."

Or, "Vacuum the floors," my mind might suggest. In alignment, I would vacuum, notice the sensations, observe the dirt, then no dirt with no judgments or criticism. I'm there, present with the task at hand. On autopilot, I might vacuum and regurgitate mentally, "I'd rather be reading. I hate this. What a waste of time. I'll just have to do this again tomorrow. Why do I have to vacuum? Why can't someone else do this? What am I going to make for dinner? I need to go to the store," and so on and so forth. It is this form of autopilot that can swiftly draw us out of alignment.

The mind is doing what it was designed to do, simplifying its input to determine the most efficient response but even though it's doing its job, it still needs a supervisor. That supervisor is your Awareness. It needs your steady, firm conscious attention of what thoughts your mind is attaching to. Once you catch the mind attaching to a thought or stream of thoughts, you can gently draw yourself back into the Alignment Zone by placing your attention on what is in front of you.

The mind was not created to automate your experiences. It was designed to automate as much as possible so that you could consciously experience the magnificence of your present reality. The Alignment Strategy helps you do that.

Awareness of LES Loops can empower you to stop yourself from moving deeper into resistance. Thoughts like, "I'd rather be reading. I hate this. What a waste of time. I'll just have to do this again tomorrow. I need to go to the grocery store," are all forms of resistance. The mind is resisting the present moment, ignoring it, choosing instead to focus on itself. The mind is resisting having to work with the heart. The mind is choosing to leave the Alignment Zone and to experience itself in the Outside Zone.

My client Joan was emotional because her mother was planning to move out of the house she owned into a retirement facility and didn't tell her about it. The two of them were at odds with each other and Joan believed that if her mother moved out, she might never hear from her mother again.

Joan was frustrated because she wanted her mother to tell her that she loved her, and to tell her she was sorry for all the pain she had caused her in the past. My client was upset because she believed that if her mother moved away, she would never hear the words, "I love you," and, therefore, would never feel loved.

Spiraling occurs when the mind triggers LES Loops and draws your attention away from the present moment. If left unattended, the mind will continue to link thoughts to more negative thoughts, trigger the emotions attached to them and pull you further and further away from the Alignment Zone. Joan was connecting the following thoughts:

- If my mother moves, I'll never hear from her again.
- If I never hear from her again, I'll never hear her tell me she loves me.
- If I never hear it, I'll feel this way forever.

- The only way to feel better is for my mother to tell me she loves me.
- My mother has never told me she loves me.
- My mother doesn't love me.
- My mother never loved me.
- My mother never did what a mother should do.
- My mother did what a mother should never do.

Joan's mind would then retrieve painful examples from her past where her mother behaved in unloving ways and play the video of it in her mind. As the video played the story of an unloving mother, it would trigger the emotional pain of feeling unloved and more and more LES Loops. The mind's automated process was what created Joan's pain, not her mother choosing to move to a retirement home.

Joan can be out of alignment and suffer as her mother moves out, or she can be in alignment and happy as her mother moves out. Either way, her mother is moving out. If my client wants to choose how she experiences her mother moving out, she needs to transform her LES Loops and move back into the Alignment Zone.

An Automated Life

Most likely up until now, your brain has been doing what it has been doing, independently, without direction from you and its sole intention has been to automate your life. It has been filtering information, finding patterns, creating loops, and determining how you should respond based on those intentions, and it may have created a false standard of alignment.

What if you stepped up and told your brain to do things differently? What if the new directive for your brain was to filter information and find patterns that optimized your Awareness of possibilities and nurtured your expansion and growth from the foundation of your natural aligned state of peace and calm? What if anything outside of that was filtered out?

The purpose of the Alignment Strategy is to draw you closer and closer to the center of the Alignment Zone by changing the filtering process. The mind is filtering anyway. Why not get it to filter in a way that serves you?

Chapter 3

PERCEPTION

Your experience of life is determined by your perception of it. You can focus on all the little parts or you can focus on the whole.

The Universe is presenting itself as the divine plan unfolding. The Universe, your body and mind, friends, family, and your circumstances are all expressions of the same divine plan. You may appear separate from me, but you and I are both expressions of the same whole.

Even though the mind creates separation by its perception of it, the mind can be trained to focus on oneness and experience life from that vantage point. It can be taught to assume that it, its experience, and everything in the Universe is a unique expression of one divine plan. When I look at you, my mind sees and interprets your body as being separate from me, but if my mind automatically scans for oneness, it sees Divinity in you. Your mind, body, experiences, the Universe, who you really are, and your reality are all expressions of oneness or the divine plan unfolding.

Your mind's decision to be in alignment with the divine plan as it unfolds will ultimately determine your experience of it.

Buried negative emotions are evidence of resistance. I saw that if I wanted to work and align myself with the divine plan, I needed to stop resisting my emotions and to allow what I was feeling to be felt, experienced, and embraced in its entirety.

I discovered that negative emotions existed because of the limiting beliefs I was believing. That meant, for each buried negative emotion within me, there was at least one negative thought that I believed to be true. By allowing myself to feel the emotions, I had the opportunity to unearth what thoughts were giving birth to them. I figured that if I knew what thoughts created the emotions, I could transform those thoughts and transform the emotions and experiences I was having. I could transform my LES Loops.

In the past, for example, my thoughts made me believe that it was the falling, my knees buckling, or maybe muscular dystrophy that was creating negative emotions. But, falling in and of itself was neither positive nor negative. For example, falling in love can be interpreted as good, while falling out of love can be seen as bad. Falling to the ground to kiss the ground I walk on often triggers positive emotion, while falling to the ground because my knees buckled tends to trigger negative emotion. The act of falling could also be seen as merely a change in position. Shifting from a standing position to a lying down position. So, it's not the experience that creates the emotions but the **interpretation** of the experience that creates them.

How does the mind do that?

The mind interprets the experience of falling by going into hyperdrive searching for connections between the available information from the experience of falling and any previous experiences, thoughts, or emotions I've ever had that were related to falling.

Instantaneously, my brain made thought connections like "not being in control of the body is bad. An uncontrolled body is weak." One thought would lead to another thought and another thought, and my Awareness or attention would be drawn upward towards my brain, away from my heart and the present moment. When my Awareness shifted like that, I'd experience a heaviness around my forehead. As soon as one of the thoughts became negative, like "not being in control of my body is bad," another form of emotional or physical discomfort would show up within me. My muscles would tense and maybe sadness would seep in. The more discomfort I experienced, the further I drifted from the Alignment Zone.

If left unattended, my mind would continue to make lightning speed connections between what "suddenly lying down" meant and other beliefs such as how lying down related to weakness, and weakness related to vulnerability, vulnerability related to not being safe, and how being unsafe was scary, and scary was connected to loneliness. My mind would spiral and trigger LES Loops. Those instantaneous mental connections would activate all the feelings I had ever felt in similar, past situations and they would penetrate and influence how I reacted in the moment. Ultimately, my response had less to do with lying on the floor after a fall and had everything to do with my mind's automatic interpretation of it.

Additionally, the emotions, weakness, and thoughts about being vulnerable, unsafe, and feeling scared were connected to other thoughts from my past, some of which were utterly unrelated to falling but were similar in emotional charge. My mind linked physical weakness to mental weakness with thoughts like, "I can't handle this. I need to be taken care of. No one will love me. I'm not loveable. It doesn't matter what I do. Everything always happens to me." All those thoughts of mental weakness would swoop in and detonate their emotional charges creating an exaggerated, patterned, ugly cry response.

But there's more. My brain would then begin searching for a solution. It would shout inside my head, "All hands on deck.

We need to stop these feelings! What can we do to relieve all this stress? Find it! It might get worse!"

Remember, the act of falling in and of itself is just an experience. When I fell in the kitchen, it was nothing more than a change in position. I moved from a standing position to a lying down position.

It was my mind that created all the emotional and mental turmoil and it was the same mind demanding that I do something about it, to take action to get rid of the stress and emotions.

It would be no different than if, upon noticing spilled milk, I got angry and responded by emptying the contents of my garbage pail on the floor, got stressed out about the mess the pail's contents created, and then worked intensely on getting it cleaned up so I could be less stressed about the mess from the pail. It all could have been prevented if I didn't empty the pail of garbage on the floor in the first place. I could have noticed the spilled milk, stayed aligned, and followed the gentle calling to wipe it up. Done. Similarly, after my fall, I could have noticed the change in position and followed the gentle calling to get back up.

That's what the Alignment Strategy is all about.

The Alignment Strategy helps you identify and transform the LES Loops that get automatically triggered and prevent you from being present and open to the gentle calling of what to do next. It keeps you in touch with your natural state, open to divine wisdom, infinite possibilities, and opportunities regardless of circumstances and without influence from past limiting beliefs or projections of the future.

When I discovered my ability to move into the Alignment Zone using The Alignment Strategy, it was no longer acceptable for me to hang out in old repetitive, negative thinking and emotions.

When I found myself lying on the kitchen floor after falling, I noticed physical and emotional signs of discomfort that indicated I had moved out of alignment. Recognizing that I moved out of alignment gave me the choice to move back in.

I affirmed, "I am supported and loved always. All my needs are taken care of. I'm safe in a house. I didn't break anything. I have clothes, food, and water."

I observed that my heart was beginning to return to its natural rhythm.

I continued to affirm, "I am having a unique divine experience. I know that this is for me. I may not know how this experience is for me but I trust in the divine plan. There is always a gift."

As I was checking things out, backside to the floor, I felt my lips form a sarcastic, little smirk, and I thought, "So, what's the gift in this?"

I drew my focus inward and noticed the cold tile beneath my body. I was supported by the floor.

I scanned the room with my eyes and I realized I had never seen my kitchen from that view before. I was growing and expanding.

My heart was beating, and I was breathing in the comfort of my own home. I was safe.

I turned my head to take in more details of the experience and there it was—another gift.

There was a spot of dirt on the baseboard. "Huh, I wouldn't have seen that if I didn't fall." I reached over, opened the cupboard door, grabbed a cloth, and wiped the dirt from the baseboard while still lying there, back pressed to the floor. What a bonus. I was able to have this unique experience and I was able to clean up a mess that would have otherwise gone unnoticed.

You might be thinking, what's the big deal about cleaning dirt off the baseboard? But it's not just about cleaning the dirt. You see, I was calm. I was peaceful. I was enjoying the experience. I was in the Alignment Zone and preventing my mind from automating my response. I still fell. I was still lying on the floor not sure how I was going to get back up. What was different was what was going on inside of me, inside my mind, inside my heart, and inside my body. **I noticed that when my thoughts were peaceful and calm, my emotions were peaceful and calm.**

I could have remained in the Outside Zone, allowed my mind to trigger LES Loops and draw me further away from the Alignment Zone. I could have cried hysterically and exhausted myself emotionally and physically as I played out all the reasons why what was happening shouldn't be happening and then got myself up again. Or, because I was training my mind to focus on oneness and experience life from that vantage point, I could recognize that I was moving out of alignment, was able to move back in, and enjoy the experience of getting back up again. The result for both would have been the same. I would have gotten back up to a standing position. What was different, however, was the journey to getting back up. One journey was exhausting, depleting, and stressful, and the other was interesting, fascinating, and actually, enjoyable.

The Alignment Strategy is a practice my clients and I use to bring ourselves back into alignment so that we can enjoy the journey, regardless of life's circumstances.

Chapter 4

SEEKING AND PROJECTION

Goal Setting

One of the biggest challenges I have experienced is keeping in Alignment while simultaneously trying to set and achieve goals. It seemed impossible to do that simultaneously.

Our society continually reminds us how we need to have goals to challenge ourselves, grow, and evolve as individuals. As a Life Coach, it is the very thing I am trained to do. I help people identify what they want, help them carve out a goal, and work with them to achieve that goal. I have found, however, that working only towards the goal can result in an empty victory.

This is why.

The very act of goal setting draws your Awareness outward to the future because it is usually done from the position that to be where you are, have what you have, be doing what you are doing is not good enough, or could be better. That analysis originates from the mind as it judges or compares your present experience to an imagined future experience, and by doing that, it draws your Awareness outward and out of Alignment. It triggers a LES Loop.

How do you stay present in the Alignment Zone while imagining what's possible in the future and setting goals?

How do you maintain a state of gratitude for what is while wanting something different?

It's all about Alignment. Are you in Alignment when you are goal setting? The answer to that can come from understanding "why you want what you want."

I have found that most clients have goals or desires based on a longing to FEEL a certain way. They hope that if they achieve their goal, they will FEEL successful, safe, appreciated, admired, proud, confident, or maybe free. They are seeking success, appreciation, and admiration. But, the act of seeking anything draws them out of Alignment. If they are not fulfilled when they are setting the goal, achieving the goal will be unfulfilling.

Seeking success comes from a limiting belief. If you seek admiration, you may have the limiting belief that you are not admired or don't deserve admiration. Limiting beliefs draw you out of Alignment because they trigger negative emotions and activate LES Loops. Any goal setting done in the outside zone will be automatically derived from lack. If your mind is no longer aligned with your heart and working alone, it will filter all available information based on your past, limiting your ability to access new, divinely-inspired ideas.

On the other hand, if you are aligned, goal setting is a divinely inspired exchange and feels like the most natural thing to do next. There is a recognition that it is not the goal itself that is important but the journey to the goal that matters. By staying in Alignment throughout the journey, you will continuously keep yourself open to divine wisdom and guidance towards your next step. Instead of creating a goal to feel successful, valued, or happy, you can choose to align with success, value, and happiness. From that aligned place, you can ask, "What goal am I being drawn to set?" By setting goals while in Alignment, success, and appreciation become the foundation for action rather than the motivation for it.

Alignment is not exclusive of doing. Alignment does not mean you don't set goals, you do nothing, or don't take action. Alignment is a state of being that provides a clear channel for what goal or next action should be taken. The goal and action are divinely inspired.

As a life coach, I have found that when a client becomes aware of the motivation behind achieving a particular goal, they either change their goal entirely or decide to make Alignment their first and only goal. By transforming the limiting beliefs drawing them out of Alignment in pursuit of a lack-based goal, they can instead draw themselves back into Alignment so they can connect with divinely inspired action and opportunities. They choose Alignment over all else so that their mind begins working with the divine plan rather than working against it.

Would it not be more enjoyable to take action, all full and complete, rather than take action to get filled up?

How would Alignment change your goal setting?

Setting Intentions

Bringing Awareness to your state of BEing before you set your intentions allows you to align yourself with who you really are, fuel the intention with love and create more loving experiences in your life.

Intentions set from the Outside Zone will create experiences of fear and lack, while intentions formed from a state of love in the Alignment Zone will create loving experiences.

While in Alignment and rooted in the heart, you can consciously be aware of your intention's purity. As Awareness, you serve, give, act, think and respond willingly and lovingly without concern for anything in return, such as recognition, monetary gain, attention, fame, advancement, safety, emotional gain, etc. Once you discover that you are setting intentions from a state of love, your state of consciousness expands and opens you up to the loving nature of your experience.

Conversely, if an intention is created from fear, the intention will be to avoid negative feelings and experiences by trying to control outside circumstances.

If the intention of giving a gift is set from a state of love, the thought of giving a gift originates out of love and given in love. That's it.

When we think of giving a gift because it is expected of us, we believe everyone else will give one, or because they gave us a gift, we are setting the intention of giving from a place of fear. Thoughts like, "I hope they like the gift. Did I spend enough? Did I spend too much? Do I have the money for this gift?" are limiting beliefs, eliciting fear, creating stress, and keeping us out of Alignment.

Bringing Awareness to the origin of our intentions can have an enormous impact on our life. If we discover that we are setting intentions from a state of fear, we can then consciously choose to draw ourselves back into Alignment where our head and heart work together and set loving intentions from there.

Three questions to ask before setting an intention.

1. What is the result I hope to achieve by setting this intention? Consider your motivation behind the intention.
2. How am I hoping to feel once I set this intention? Consider whether or not you have any expectations.
3. Am I trying to control the outcome or am I unattached to the outcome?

By bringing Awareness to your state of BEing before you set your intentions, you can align yourself with who you really are, fuel the intention with love and create more loving experiences in your life.

The Allure of The Spiritual High

Spiritual practices, experiences, conferences, theories, and groups may be just another way your mind keeps you focused on the outer world.

If I wonder if this person can help me go deeper or if this group will help me connect more, I remind myself that "more" is impossible. Going deeper assumes there is a level, some benchmark measuring my spiritual attainment. It's like trying to rank my ability to be Lori when I am already a Lori. I can't be more or less of a Lori. Similarly, we can't rate our spirituality. We already are spiritual, in its entirety, and nothing we do or say can change that. We already are the best version of ourselves. It is only our mind that makes us believe otherwise by the limiting beliefs it's believing.

The longing for more or the desire to recreate a euphoric feeling represents our state of Awareness and not our level of spiritual enlightenment. A desire for more suggests that what you have now is not enough, and "not enough" is a limiting belief. Any limiting belief or negative feeling indicates that our Awareness is focused on an outside experience to fill an emotional longing or sense of disconnection.

Those on the spiritual path are not immune to the mind's desire to draw Awareness outwards. It masks itself brilliantly as an energetic surge during meditation, a mystical experience, a physiological tingling, emotional shift, or collection of knowledge that is perceived as something done or achieved. The simple desire to recreate it is drawing you outwards because it perpetuates the illusion that pleasure is derived from an experience and doesn't already intrinsically exist.

Any feeling of less than or more than is an indication that our Awareness is focused on the outer world and we are no longer in Alignment with our true selves. Feeling the desire to instruct others (more than), believing a manifestation is of your own doing (more than), superiority (more than), seeing oneself as being special (more than), evolved (more than), needing guidance (less than), not there yet (less than), separate (less than), are all indicators that limiting beliefs are active.

When I notice that I am focused on the outside world, I consciously draw my Awareness inward and ask myself, what am I believing that is drawing my focus outward?

For example, once I had a strong desire to travel to Europe for a week-long retreat to see a guru. By questioning my intent, I identified that my desire stemmed from my belief that he would help me go deeper in my understanding of who I really am. I believed that he knew more than I did, he had more abilities than me, that he was special, he had the power to create changes within me, and it would be faster to go to him than to wait for my own insight. I was looking for him to fulfill my need to feel satisfied, unique, gifted, transformed, connected, and loved.

Instead, I affirmed, "I know everything I need to know in this moment. No one has more abilities or knowledge than what lies within me. Everyone is unique. Only I have the power to create change within me. Insight is who I am and it's only my belief that I'm not that, that is keeping me from accessing it." I then thanked the Universe for the experience to work on a limiting belief and the opportunity to move back into the Alignment Zone.

It can be tricky to discern spiritual insight from the emotional and physical euphoric charge sometimes created from seeking behavior. Seeking behaviors are actions taken to get more, acquire more, experience more, attain more than what we already have in the moment. Those behaviors draw us out of Alignment.

I thought I was aligned and connected to my inner wisdom when I was being called to go to Europe but through deeper reflection and Awareness, the feeling of being called to go there was instead a subtle longing for more than what I already had. It was an alarm bell letting me know I was leaving the Alignment Zone and that the limiting belief, "I need/want to be more enlightened," was drawing my Awareness outward. Trying to find an easier, faster way to be enlightened was my mind's strategy of keeping me busy DOing or seeking, and kept my Awareness outwardly focused in the Outside Zone.

It doesn't mean we can't go to see practitioners, read books, or receive treatments to support our spiritual journey. I have read many books, sat in many audiences, and participated in plenty of workshops and they all helped me understand metaphysics, positive psychology, and my spiritual journey. However, what truly transformed my experience was the personal application of the teachings, every day, as often as possible until it became my new habit. When the teachings became ingrained, I was able to notice even the subtlest of changes in how I felt physiologically, mentally, and emotionally. By recognizing those changes, I could intentionally keep myself in the Alignment Zone, move back into it when I noticed I strayed and transform any limiting beliefs that were behind the moving in and out.

Chapter 5

RESISTANCE

The Questions You Are Asking

I discovered that my brain seemed to ask questions that were always focused on all the negatives amid a challenge. It was as though I was wearing a pair of glasses made of lack, and they were only allowing into view what was lacking or needing to change so that I could get back to the status quo or into my comfort zone.

My brain would ask, "What am I losing?" and the glasses would filter the experience zeroing in on the losses. How is this going to make things worse? How is my life going to be less than what it was before this happened?

I saw everything through the eyeglasses of lack. With each question, I would move further and further into resistance and away from my aligned state. The further into resistance I would go, the more LES Loops got triggered. My mind would conjure up all the negatives of how what was happening shouldn't be happening and create a projected future of doom and gloom.

For instance, when I was nineteen and in the middle of my first set of exams in University, I had this unbearable pain in the center of my back, so I made an appointment to see the doctor on campus.

One appointment led to another, and I found myself in his office, across from him, when I heard him say, "you have Muscular Dystrophy."

I saw his lips moving, I knew he was talking, but I couldn't take it in. I struggled to get home, my head swarming with images of a dilapidated body slumped in a wheelchair, unable to move and communicate. I thought my life was over. I was filtering the experience through the lens of loss and lack, seeing the images created by the mind's questions. What am I losing? How is this going to make my life worse?

I realize now that if I want to stay aligned during a perceived challenge, I need to start asking different questions. Instead of asking, "What am I losing? I need to ask, "What am I gaining?" Instead of asking, "Why is this happening to me? I need my brain to ask, "How is this for me? Instead of asking, "What is being taken away from me? I need to ask, "What gifts am I receiving?"

So that's what I did. I began rewiring my brain. I began retraining it to make the automatic assumption that the following conditions always exist in every moment.

Life happens for me.

There is a gift.

I am safe.

I am whole.

I am loved and supported, always.

I am the divine plan observing the divine plan unfolding.

And instead of scanning the carnage of a challenge in a state of fear looking for lack or loss, I began exploring my situation with curiosity, looking for what might be gained. "How am I supported, loved, growing, expanding, evolving in this moment?" I would continue to ask those questions and sit with my answers until I began moving back into the Alignment

Zone. Just like I did when I fell on the kitchen floor and at the pool. I looked for gifts and drew my Awareness inward until I realigned myself with my natural state of peace and calm.

I invite you to consider then, that you too, always have a choice. Even if you are lying on the floor trying to figure out how to get up again, interacting in a relationship, struggling at work, or dealing with money, that you get to choose what questions to ask. You can look for what's wrong or missing and move out into the Outside Zone, or you can chill, lay back, glance out from your view in the Alignment Zone, and get your brain to start asking different questions. Instead of asking what are you losing, get your brain to consider what are you gaining? Instead of asking why is this happening to you, ask, how is this for you? Instead of asking what is being taken away, ask what gifts are you receiving?

Before you know it, you'll be living in the Alignment Zone, aligned with your true nature where you naturally assume that life happens for you and that there is a gift in every moment. You'll be perceiving life from the state of being where your mind will naturally gravitate to thoughts that assume you are safe, whole, loved and supported, always. That's when the undercurrent of possibility replaces the fear, and peace, calm, and clarity become the foundation of your experience. So much so, that you no longer will have to ask the questions, because you'll notice the gifts right away.

The Power of Language

Words in and of themselves are just letters. Letters are lines. Lines are ink. Therefore words, by themselves will not influence your movement out of the Alignment Zone, but the meaning you attach to them will.

When we were born, we didn't know words existed. As we were exposed to a new term, we learned its meaning based on our experiences with them. The word Mom, for instance, had no significance until our mind made a connection between the experiences we were having with our Mother and the word Mom. Each new experience would expand our understanding and definition of what she was.

Words are powerful. Each word can move you in and out of the Alignment Zone based on the meaning you have attached to it. If you had a loving relationship with your Mother, the word Mom probably would have little impact on your Alignment. If you had an abusive childhood, the word Mom might conjure up negative experiences and draw you out of the Alignment Zone.

TELL ME ABOUT YOURSELF

"Tell me about yourself," someone asked.

"I was born in a small town, and my father died when I was thirteen, followed by my Mother dying with cancer when I was 18. I then went to University and was diagnosed with Muscular Dystrophy when I was 19. I graduated from teacher's college, got married, had a miscarriage and a stroke by 26. I had to quit my job at 29 because of the pain and weakness caused by my Muscular Dystrophy, and I've been homesick ever since," I replied.

As I write that paragraph for this book, I can feel the pull to leave the Alignment Zone. It feels depressing, stressful, and heavy because my mind tries to make connections to old limiting beliefs.

When I first became aware of this mental list of who I thought I was, I was shocked. No wonder I felt lethargic and depressed. If that was the dialogue I was having and the thoughts I was believing, I was living detached from the true nature of who I was in the Outside Zone. The definition of who I believed myself to be was so far from the truth that the separation was causing me to suffer.

My mind unconsciously processed the vocabulary I was using, and the story kept me out of Alignment with my true nature.

I uncovered that the unconscious intention behind me telling the painful story of what I had been through. If people knew my story, they might understand me, the pain would subside, and I would get some relief.

I see now that there was nothing anyone could have said or done to make me feel better. My pain was created by the words used in my dialogue, triggering my limiting beliefs, negative emotions, and outdated strategies.

Not only was I telling the story with words that drew me out of Alignment, but I was also rehashing the story in my head with vivid, video-like detail. Father dying, Mother dying, miscarriage, stroke, sick. My strategy of telling my painful story to feel "understood" was actually creating more suffering.

I wanted other people to understand me but I did not understand me. I did not understand that I was the one creating my pain by the story I was telling. I didn't understand that I was responsible for how I was feeling and how I was feeling, was determined by my Alignment or lack thereof. It was not the death of my parents, a health diagnosis, or a change in physical ability that defined how I felt, but my thoughts and the words I used to think and talk about it. I was creating my reality by my perception of it.

It didn't matter what response someone gave me because I would never get the relief I was looking for. The relief I was looking for could have only been found by me moving back into Alignment. Changing my verbal and mental dialogue was an essential first step to transforming my limiting beliefs and moving back into the Alignment Zone.

I could have replied, "I was born in a small town, my father was a police officer and my mother was a bookkeeper. I went to University, graduated from teacher's college, got married, and had two children. I was a stay-at-home mom and have been on a journey back to my true self ever since." The vocabulary in that response was more neutral and had fewer negative emotional and experiential attachments. The more neutral the thoughts, the less power they have to draw me out of Alignment and trigger LES Loops.

If I am in Alignment, the story of me begins with the understanding that everything that happened should have happened, and all that happened was essential for me to be me, the way I am now in this moment. The divine plan played out precisely the way it was intended to play out. When I am in the Alignment Zone, I also understand that any story of what happened to me is only one story, one version, of thousands that could be told. I am aware that I am sharing one perceptual version of many and remain open to alternate versions as well. That openness is indicative of being aligned.

Where in your life are you only perceiving one version of what happened to you?

Alignment feels loving, calm, and peaceful. In the Alignment Zone, strategies are not required, and your response follows the gentle urge to do what seems loving. It may be to tell a story of your past or maybe, not to share at all.

The most loving thing you can do for yourself and others is to bring yourself back into Alignment. Once you are back in Alignment, you can observe what is happening and be a silent witness to your experience without a story. It creates the space to choose your words and determine your most aligned response.

THE G WORD

How is the term "God" experienced within you?

What happened when you read the first sentence of this section or came across the word God throughout this book?

How do you react when people use the word God, you hear it during a television show, or someone talks about their faith?

I had a friend that said she cringed and folded up into herself the minute someone said the G-word, yet this same friend was committed to her spiritual unfoldment, growth, and expansion. "I grew up in a very religious household filled with memories of daily bible reading and condemnation. I feel so angry when I hear that word. I prefer using the term Universe," she said.

The word God has evolved based on your mind's interpretation of its experiences with the term God over time. For one friend, the name God was associated with condemnation, and each time she heard the word, her mind connected to the beliefs, emotions, and experiences from her past of condemnation. As an adult, I experienced the term God with embarrassment, struggled to speak it, and stumbled when I read it. My experience with God as an adult was a reflection of my experience of God as a child.

When I began my spiritual journey, I signed up for a Spiritual University program. I didn't intend to do anything with it, so imagine my surprise when I discovered that the program's successful completion gave me the qualifications to be ordained as a Metaphysical Minister in Ontario. It seemed the whole process just sort of swept me up, and before I knew it, I was being ordained in a public ceremony. Another student who was being ordained at the same time was incredibly proud and invited her entire family to attend the event. I recall observing her and being in awe of her enjoyment of it.

I didn't tell any of my friends or family about the ordination because deep down I felt embarrassed and believed that I didn't know enough about God to be ordained.

Whether or not I knew enough or didn't know enough about God to be ordained was irrelevant. What was relevant was my belief that "I didn't know enough" because that belief drew me away from the Alignment Zone and away from my natural state of peace and calm into old triggered emotional responses of embarrassment. I did know enough about God to be ordained because I was, in that moment, being ordained. That was my reality at that moment. My experience of that ordination had nothing to do with my knowledge of God and everything to do with my Alignment with God.

If I were in Alignment with God, I would have been aligned with the divine perfection of what was. I would have embraced the unfoldment of the moment, trusted in its rightness, and observant of its beauty. I may have invited friends and family and enjoyed the experience. That was available to me but hidden behind the limiting beliefs of my childhood past.

I grew up Presbyterian. After pulling on scratchy leotards and an itchy dress, my sister and I would walk down to the end of the road and wait for Mr. Pengwarden, an elder at the church, to pick us up. We'd climb in the back seat and smooth out our dresses as he drove us across town.

My church and God experience was a sense of "not understanding what people were talking about." I never understood the Minister's sermons, and in Sunday school, I often felt embarrassed because I didn't really grasp the concepts or how to look up the passages. The discomfort was reinforced by the other girls in class who giggled and distanced themselves at the other end of the table.

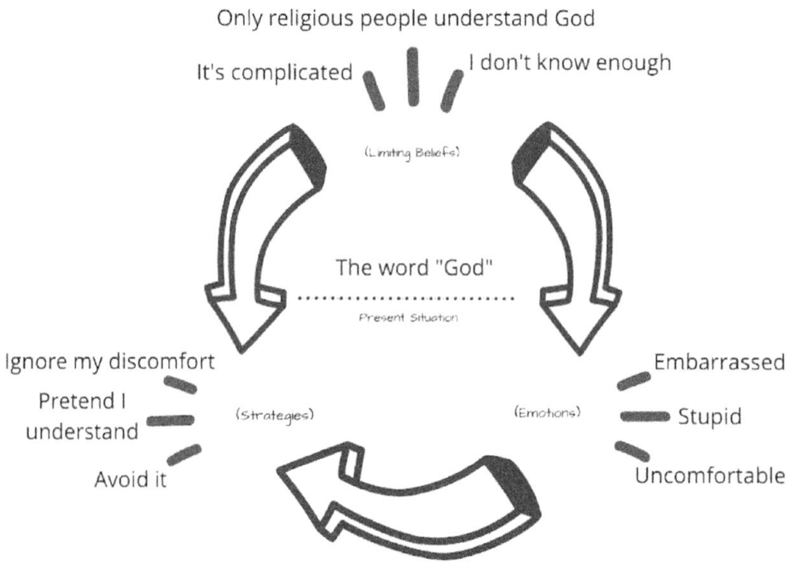

By transforming my limiting beliefs about the church and God, I recognized that I understood exactly what I was supposed to understand as a child at church and did the best that I could do at the time. Now I can appreciate that the Minister did his best, and the Sunday school teacher was a volunteer and did her best too. As an adult, I can see that even though those giggling girls had their own Bibles, they didn't understand what it said neither because if they had, they wouldn't have giggled, distanced themselves, and made fun of me in class.

For me, the process of transforming the limiting beliefs I had about God included using alternate words in place of the term God. I used the name Universe and sometimes even "peanut butter" to refer to my new experiences with spirituality to prevent myself from being drawn out of Alignment. Once I was comfortable with my new relationship with God,

I used the term Universe interchangeably. Now the word God no longer triggers old beliefs and emotions or draws me out of Alignment. I still have memories of going to church and the giggling girls, but those memories have lost their power to draw me out of Alignment.

The Alignment Strategy brings Awareness to what is drawing you away from aligning with your natural loving state and creates the opportunity to transform it. It does not matter what you call your natural loving state but only that you know it always exists and that it doesn't require a name.

The Need for Control

I had a client who was exhausted. As a self-proclaimed control freak, she insisted that being in control was necessary because when she stopped trying to figure things out, it was disastrous. In our session, we identified that the predominant limiting belief that was preventing her from achieving her goal of being OK with what is, was that she believed, "if she were not in control, her life would be a disaster."

On the one hand, she wanted to live life in a state of allowing, to trust that what was happening, should be happening. She wanted to live life from the Alignment Zone. On the other hand, she had this powerful belief that to let go, to stop trying to figure things out would result in a disastrous life.

Her goal, therefore, was in complete opposition to her belief system.

When my client was a little girl, she always got what she wanted. If she went to her Mother and her Mother said no, she would go to her grandmother, who always said yes. She associated a no or not getting what she wanted with a negative or lousy feeling and associated a yes, or getting what she wanted with a positive or good feeling. By never being denied anything as a child, she became accustomed to getting what she wanted.

Her mind made the connection that, "If I get what I want, I'll be happy." She learned to attribute her happiness to something that happened outside of herself and that she could control it.

She did not recognize the happiness that existed within her before she looked outward to get a yes.

Believing her happiness was something to be acquired, she created strategies to ensure she got a yes in the outside world. As a safety net, she also created a strategy for the possibility of not getting what she wanted, and that was to abandon what she was doing and create a new project or goal. As an adult, when there is a risk of not getting what she wants, she abandons what she is working on, leaving a long trail of unfinished projects.

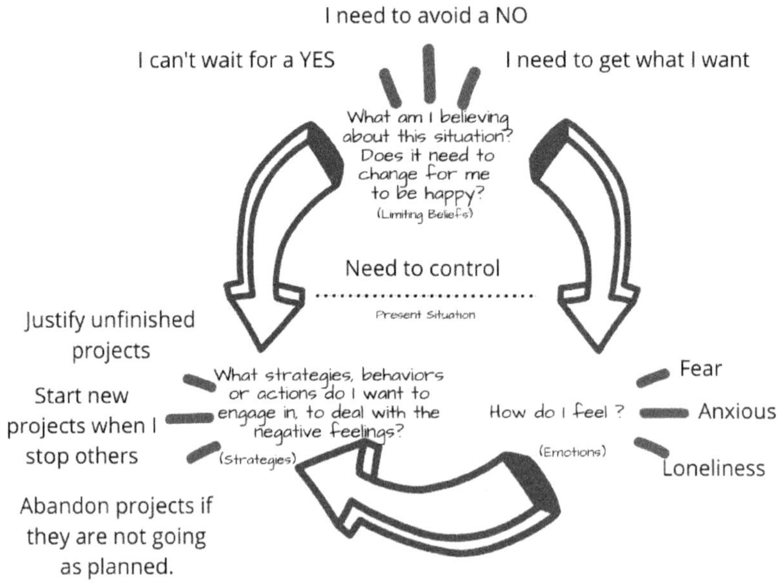

However, her happiness experience by getting a "yes" is not the same as the happiness experienced in the Alignment Zone.

If she was aligned, she would trust that getting a "no" would be the perfect response in that moment and there would be no need for control. She would be open to the gentle, inward guidance as to what to do next, and she would recognize that any circumstances outside of her could not change her natural state or who she really was.

This client grew up never having considered the perspective that "no," could be a positive. Therefore, her brain didn't have proof that being told no or something not working out as planned could be a good thing.

Some would say that not accepting a "no" is a sign of someone who is determined and perseveres but, "To not accept a no" actually creates resistance in the present moment. The belief that an experience is not acceptable is an example of resistance and draws you out of Alignment. It's not "the moving forward with an alternate action" that creates misalignment but the state of origin where the action was initiated that creates misalignment.

If getting a "no," creates discomfort, responding from that state of discomfort creates an action born out of resistance. The actions taken to get a yes from a misaligned place create more misalignment or further resistance. If she were using the Alignment Strategy, she would recognize her discomfort, move back into the Alignment Zone and go inward to recognize the gentle calling of what next action, if any, she should take.

If we take action when we are out of Alignment, we are taking action to relieve the discomfort of being out of Alignment. When we are out of Alignment, any action creates more of what it was birthed from, lack and resistance. This keeps LES Loops looping.

Aligned action feels good before, during, and after. If she were aligned and getting divine guidance, she would have been **drawn towards what action to take next, with no attachment to the outcome and in a state of continued fullness rather**

than moving away from the discomfort or moving towards pleasure.

Most limiting beliefs go unnoticed and continuously trigger automatic responses unless we intentionally become aware of whether or not we are aligned. If we practice bringing Awareness to how we feel emotionally and physically, we can use that information to recognize when we are moving out of Alignment before we get too far out in the Outside Zone. It takes less effort to catch ourselves when we are moving out of Alignment than it does to wait until we're so far out it seems impossible to get ourselves back into the Alignment Zone.

Another client of mine also had the belief that she needed to be in control. For her, controlling her behaviors, emotions, and responses was critical for her to feel good. She was careful to screen what she shared with others and kept any information that could potentially portray her as being weak or not good enough to herself. My client was also careful to behave in a way that she believed others wanted her to behave to gain their approval and affection. Her unconscious limiting belief was that if I do, say, and act the way others want me to, they'll love me, and in turn... I'll feel loved. Her strategy of holding back, screening her actions, emotions, and communications with herself and others had unknowingly kept her in a constant state of underlying stress and misalignment. She was living life with the brakes on.

If she were in the Alignment Zone, there would be no need for control. She would be open, expressive, and loving all of herself, unconcerned with others' opinions.

This client assured me that she meditated, repeated affirmations, exercised, and had a balanced life. Still, all that was not enough to draw the client back into Alignment because the limiting belief that she needed to have control was so emotionally charged and became such an embedded pattern of behavior that kept her in the Outside Zone in a false state of

Alignment. By working with her to identify the LES Loop, she moved back into Alignment and let go of the need to control reality.

THE WALL

Frequently, clients refer to having a wall up to protect their feelings in a bid to keep themselves safe or protected from being hurt. The wall is a strategy devised by the mind to keep them from feeling a certain way and, in this case, hurt. It's another form of control.

Let's use a LES Loop and break it down.

The limiting beliefs in this instance might be, "I need to protect myself, I need to control my feelings, and I can't share my feelings.

The emotions that get triggered when those limiting beliefs are active could be fear, anxiety, and caution, and the strategies might be not to share their feelings, don't express what they are thinking, and keep themselves on guard.

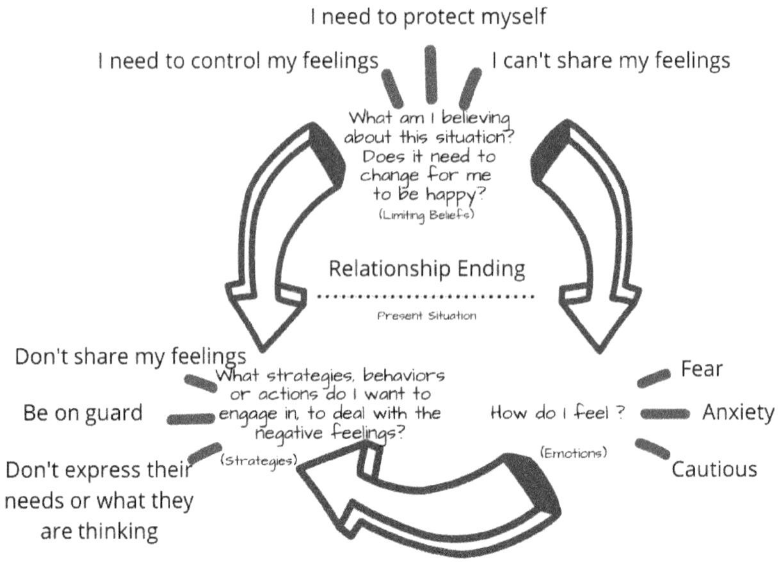

If, for example, the intention is to put up a wall between yourself and another person to keep yourself from being hurt, then that strategy of putting up a wall will automatically come into play when you make yourself vulnerable.

In this case, the wall you put up to keep yourself emotionally distant will be the same wall that will keep you from the intimacy you crave.

If you believe you will be hurt, your mind will look for evidence that you are being hurt or could be hurt. If you believe you are unsafe, your mind will look for evidence that you are unsafe. Your mind will screen the experiences you are having with the other person by filtering and discarding information about how they are loving, kind, trustworthy, and dependable and instead focus on information about how they can hurt you. That process keeps the LES Loop, looping and creates fear and anxiety. It has nothing to do with other people.

By not sharing your feelings, you're holding back, moving out of Alignment, and resisting your true nature to love and be loved.

The limiting beliefs and the strategies you use to keep yourself safe are actually keeping you from seeing another person's loving nature and blocking you from sharing the true essence of who you are with them.

To feel safe, loved, and loving, you must transform the LES Loops that moved you out of Alignment and created the wall in the first place. Once back in the Alignment Zone, you will be aligned with your loving nature, full, whole, and complete just as you are. In that state, other people can't hurt you because you won't believe they can. If there are no active LES Loops, love just fills you up and expands so readily; you can't help but let it flow uncontrollably out and into your relationships and experiences.

Illness

When I was nineteen, I was diagnosed with FSH Muscular Dystrophy (MD), a genetic, slowly, progressive muscle disorder that turns muscle into fat. There is no treatment or cure.

As a result of MD, I have experienced the slow deterioration of my muscles since 1980, noticeable mostly by the activities that I am no longer able to do. My healthy muscles or the ones that are not yet affected tend to compensate for those I lose, so the impact of a lost muscle sometimes goes undetected until it affects some sort of daily activity. For instance, not being able to raise my arms above my head resulted in me not playing volleyball. When I lost the muscles in my leg or foot, walking became difficult. In-between these changes were plateau periods where I could adapt my environment, learn to accept my new set of circumstances, and continue on with my life.

This process of experiencing loss, grief, and accepting it, happened each time I experienced muscle loss.

When I could no longer play sports, I'd grieve the loss of that part of my life and accept my new circumstances. I'd suck it up and move on. When I could no longer pick up my children, I'd grieve that physical loss, let go of the Mother I wanted to be, and learn to accept that too. Then when I could no longer walk properly, I'd grieve and accept that, and so on.

I was exhausted. I was in a constant state of grieving, and it was depressing. Even if I was in a state of acceptance, I was still stressed out because I anticipated my next form of loss. I thought, "This process can't possibly be what I was put on this earth to experience. There has to be a better way."

In the year 2000, I heard about The Law of Attraction and how I could heal my life by changing my thoughts. I was skeptical at first, but I dove into the spiritual teachings hoping to figure out exactly what I needed to do to heal my body. I figured that if I did what the teachings told me to do, I would be able to heal my body, live in a state of peace and calm, and live a normal life.

When I began my spiritual journey, I focused on positive affirmations, the negative thoughts I was having, and I started to change my vocabulary. I felt great, and it validated for me that the spiritual stuff did work. Inspired to learn more, I dove in deeper, reading, studying, attending workshops, and so on. My life did change, and my health improved too. I was able to gain strength, had less pain, and a lot more energy. I was thrilled.

Until I lost my ability to climb stairs.

I was expecting to be healed, and when my muscles deteriorated further, I was crushed. I had invested in the belief that if my body was healed, I would be happy. I was seeking happiness and I was destined to be disappointed because I was out of Alignment the minute I sought a healthy body.

A goal formed in unhappiness results in unhappiness.

This is why.

I was repeating positive affirmations, exercising, and reading self-development books to heal my body so I could be happy. That meant I was out of Alignment when I set the goal. I was projecting and seeking happiness based on my body's abilities. My actions were rooted in the belief that if I do this, I'll get that. I believed that if I repeated positive affirmations and stopped using negative words, my body would heal and go back to the way it was before the Muscular Dystrophy took hold. I believed that if my body went back to normal, I'd be happy.

The affirmations were moving me towards the Alignment Zone, but because I was seeking happiness by achieving or changing something, I remained in the Outside Zone.

If I am needing or wanting something beyond what I have, I am not in Alignment. Even though I began to feel better, I was not aligned but instead, was experiencing a false state of Alignment. This was noticeable by my investment in my body's abilities and my devastation triggered by further deterioration.

It was the expectation of my body being healed that resulted in my devastation.

I couldn't want something different than what I already had and be in Alignment at the same time

I can almost hear you saying, "What? Can't I want anything? Can't I have goals? I can't have a desire or I'll be out of Alignment?"

I noticed that the more I worked on my ability to love what is to stay in Alignment, the more easily I could recognize the smallest of expectations I was having. Eventually, after repeatedly going through the loss, grief, acceptance process and simultaneously working on loving what is, I could see that the number and size of expectations I was having were decreasing, and so was my suffering.

As I began transforming my limiting beliefs, moving closer and closer to the Alignment Zone, my needs and desires to want anything other than what I had, decreased. I was experiencing more of my natural state of happiness and therefore needed less of it to come from outside of me.

My sensitivity to discomfort became so fine-tuned that I began to spot the slightest sign of an active expectation or seeking type of thought or behavior as it arose throughout my day.

Is it possible to stay in Alignment and want something different?

ILLNESS AND THE LAW OF ATTRACTION

Thousands use the Law of Attraction as a way to manifest what they want. It suggests that you;

1. Identify what you don't want
2. Identify what you do want
3. Imagine having what it is you want.

If you do those things, you'll manifest what you want.

Consider this.

Step one moves me out of Alignment. I'm resisting what I have.

Step two moves me out of Alignment. I am seeking more, to be happy.

Step three moves me into Alignment. I am happy with what is.

Why not just stay aligned and love what I have? It seems more loving to stay in Alignment with my true self, pure unconditional love, and my natural state of peace, calm, and happiness, rather than move out of that, just to turn around and move myself back into Alignment to be happy. What a waste of energy, time, effort, and a whole lot of unnecessary suffering.

"But I create my experience." I thought. "How can I create my experience without changing anything. If I don't create anything, everything will be the same."

If I don't create anything, everything will be the same? Is that true?

If I just sat there and never moved would everything stay the same?

I had this flashback to the funeral of my father when I was 13. As I sat in the back seat of one of the funeral procession cars, I stared out the window at people exiting the grocery store, walking, holding hands on the sidewalk, and cars passing us going the opposite way. I wanted them to stop. I wanted them to understand what had happened to me, and I wanted them to stop because my life had stopped. But, life just kept on being lived.

Life lives. It lives if I think I am creating it, and it lives if I think I am not creating it.

That was it. That's when I understood that it is only a belief that I am the one creating reality by what I do, say, or think.

I had the belief that I could manipulate outside circumstances, my body included, to be something other than what it is. I had the belief that a body without MD was preferable. No matter how I tried to create, I could not create without moving out of Alignment first. Because, by taking ownership of creation, my ownership created misalignment.

"Look. Look what I did. I am special. I manifested that. I'm better than you."

I created my experience not by how I was changing or creating reality but by how I perceived it.

To heal me, I needed to transform the belief that I needed healing because it was my perception that needed healing, not my body. If I believe I don't need healing, then I am OK with my body or loving what is. If I love what is, I'm in the Alignment Zone. If I am in the Alignment Zone, I am believing, feeling, experiencing my natural state of unconditional love, happiness, peace, and calm.

I can't love everything unconditionally and have a preference for something else.

If I were in Alignment and loved everything, including my body with MD, I would love my MD body.

I began exploring my MD body with curiosity asking, "How am I supported, evolving in this moment because I am experiencing this body with Muscular Dystrophy?"

What am I gaining? How is this experience for me? How am I growing and expanding? What is the gift in this?

I recognized that I had the belief that not having MD was better than having it. Therefore, I was telling God that the divine plan was wrong, that I knew better, and that I should not have MD.

If I were in Alignment, I would have understood that MD is something I needed because I had it. There are no mistakes with the divine plan. I can't think that we are all one, pure love and then, find an exception.

My thought can be in Alignment with all that is, or not. There is not a thought that can be kinda, sorta in Alignment. A thought can completely, wholly, align with the true essence of who I am, who you are, as one with all that is, or not. My thoughts can be aligned or not aligned. I can choose to believe that life happens for me. I can choose to believe that there is always a gift. I am safe. I am whole. I am loved and supported, always. The divine plan is unfolding. Everything is as it should be. Everything that is, is necessary. There are no exceptions when I am aligned. I create my experience by the thoughts I have about it. I am grateful for the MD diagnosis because it is the experience that brought me to this deep understanding of the Alignment Zone.

There was a practitioner who once questioned, "What if you got the lesson or experience from having the MD and you no longer need it? Can you not heal the body to match your new spiritual understanding, so you can serve and help more people?"

If I have it, I need it. There are no exceptions. When I understand that what I have, is what I need, then I know I have exactly what I need in every moment.

As soon as I have the thought, I got a lesson and no longer need the MD; those words that make up that thought draw me out of Alignment. The vocabulary is negative. The term "lesson" assumes I knew less than what I know now. "I needed a lesson" resonates with inferiority like a child vs. parent or teacher.

"I no longer need MD" is a thought that argues with reality and creates suffering. If I believe I don't need something that I have, I'm trying to change reality by getting rid of it, and that draws me out of Alignment into resistance.

If I am supposed to help more people, more people will come into my experience for help. If I need to have a body without MD to do that, then I will have a body without MD.

I know that for over 20 years if I could have dodged doing the inner work, I would have. It was having the MD and my inability to escape it that brought me my freedom. The Universe created an experience for me that was repeatedly being asked to be dealt with. I couldn't ignore it. I couldn't go out or work to avoid doing the inner work. The inner work was what I was supposed to do, and the Universe created the perfect circumstances for it to occur. How do I know this? I know this because my inner work is what was done.

Until the last five years, I was moving through life mostly in the Outside Zone, continually searching and grasping for anyone and anything that could show me how I could heal my body. I read the books, attended conferences, went on retreats, and studied hard. I practiced meditation, learned Reiki, and taught classes, all in the pursuit of healing my body so I could change my experience.

On the one hand, I was doing everything I could to move back into the Alignment Zone, but on the other hand, I had a deep resistance to having MD.

It wasn't until I had an unwavering belief that there are no exceptions to the understanding that we are and our lives are the perfect unfoldment of the divine plan. No modifications are needed. No matter how it is in the moment, my body is the unflawed unfoldment of the divine plan.

My only job is to enjoy that flawlessness, and I can do that in the Alignment Zone.

NARROW PERCEPTIONS

There were two ways to walk with my walker down the hallway to my condo. The first way kind of went like this.

"Man, I am tired. It has been such a long day."

I hate having to concentrate on every step. I can't stand making sure I'm taking my time, lifting my foot, placing it securely in front of me, and regaining my balance each time, while I fiercely grip the handles of my walker. My stressful thoughts are jumping in, between each next step.

In my mind, I imagine people looking, wondering what is wrong with me, and how grateful they are that they are not me.

These thoughts keep jamming their way into my head. I want to be the woman that walks. I want you to feel comfortable when you meet me, to see ME and not the walker. I want to be a powerful mother, the vibrant, outgoing friend you knew, and the free-spirited woman my husband married.

I want everything to change. My body, this disease, my stress, my relationships, other people.

Or, the second way to walk with my walker down the hallway to my condo kinda goes like this.

I notice my body, how it feels. I'm so grateful for all that it did today, and I will sit down when I get home so it can rest. This walker is terrific. It supports my movement forward, helps me balance, carries my purse, and rolls along so easily on the carpet.

Mmmm. I smell Italian. Somebody must be cookin' up a storm behind one of these numbered doors. The crystal wall scones cast the gentlest light, leading me home. I notice the warmth from my winter coat. What a great coat.

My thoughts are flowing in and out. How marvelous to be this woman walking, supported down the hallway, warm and happy.

And then it happens.

My toe catches the rug, creating enough resistance for me to lose my balance and fall forward, my upper body hovering over the top of the walker and my hands desperately holding on, sandwiched between the handles of the walker and the weight of my body pressing down on them.

I don't have the strength to straighten myself up. Here I thought I would walk down the hallway and enter my condo like I usually did but instead, this. Who knew? What an adventure.

There were two ways to walk down the hallway, but now, there is a third! This third way was to walk only partway.

Right now, I'm this. A woman bent over, hugging a walker in a hallway with no one around.

Now what?

I make a fruitless attempt to straighten. That's not happening. I consider my options as I glance ahead at my condo door five feet away. Even if I shimmy over there, I won't be able to release the grip on the walker to turn the doorknob. That won't work.

I could fall to the ground and try to open the door that way, but I'm afraid I won't be able to reach it. I can't believe this is happening to me. This is so embarrassing.

I hear the faint dinging of my neighbor's dog tag. Maybe, if I can get close enough, I can knock the top of my head on his door and see if he can help me straighten up.

I don't want this. I want to be the woman who walks, the woman I was, the woman you knew, the woman you hoped I'd be. Anything, but the woman bent over, hugging a walker in a hallway with no one around.

I've now managed to get close enough to my neighbor's unit, and I rock slightly so that the top of my head gently taps his door. Their dog barks, and I'm relieved, he heard me.

But no one comes.

I suddenly realize that they probably did come, but looked out the peephole and didn't see anyone because I was bent over out of view. I can't help but chuckle. Is this really happening?

I gently tap my head against the door again. The dog barks.

This time my neighbor answers. As the door opens, slippered feet come into view, and I imagine his shocked and confused expression as he takes in what's before him. A woman bent over, hugging a walker in the hallway.

"Can you help me straighten up?" I asked. And he did.

That's it. I'm done. This is not working for me. I need to do something different. I'm getting a wheelchair.

I don't care that you think I should keep walking, that I don't meet your projections of who you think I am or what I should be doing. I don't care that my brain is yelling at me not to do it. What will people think? Your life will be over...

I am going to let go of the woman who walks, the woman I was, the woman you knew, the woman you hoped I'd be, the woman I hoped I'd be, and embrace and love this woman, just as she is, right here, right now.

I'm going to love her all over, all of her, just as she is, and choose to do whatever it takes to nurture and support her.

I got a wheelchair. (Mind blown hand action and sound) OMG. My whole world opened up. I could do what I wanted to do, go where I wanted to go. I no longer had to worry about falling, tripping, or getting tired.

All this mental space opened up. Instead of processing all these thoughts up in my head, I could now tune into what was happening out there, around me, and in me. I became intimately engaged with life.

What I had projected to be the worst possible thing that could happen, being bent over a walker, banging the top of my head-on neighbor's door, turned out to be the best possible thing that could happen. Because, just like my neighbor looking out the peephole at a narrow view of all that was outside his door, I too had a narrow view of what was possible for me if I couldn't walk like everyone else.

It made me realize I had a choice. I could move through life, holding on for dear life, fearful of every step, bracing for impact OR, I could consider how what was happening should be happening. That what was happening was FOR me. It's an opportunity for me to grow and expand so I can be the powerful, vibrant, outgoing, free-spirited woman I am meant to be.

I recalibrated my future of what was possible by opening up to alternate possibilities of how to take my next step. I considered that my life was going to be so amazing, so magnificent, so out of this world, beyond anything I could ever dream possible, that, for me take it all in and get ready for it,...the Universe was saying, "Girlfriend, you better sit down for this."

I lived life with the narrow perception that walking was the only way I could be happy. That was until that crazy experience broke me open and created a tiny space where the alternate perception that "getting a wheelchair would be a good idea" could seep in.

I realized that Muscular Dystrophy, my body, had nothing to do with my happiness. The muscular dystrophy, my body, were doing what they were meant to be doing, and I was having an experience with it. How I chose to perceive that experience determined how happy or sad I was.

Was I in the Alignment Zone, seeing the gifts and trusting that no matter how terrifying the moment could be, it might be the very experience I needed to evolve into the woman I was meant to be? Or was I in the Outside Zone wearing glasses of lack? Was I spending all my energy wanting to be a woman who walks? Was I focused on how other people walked, worked, played, dug in their garden, kayaked, and how I didn't? Was I only noticing how my body was not walking, falling short, not good enough, wrong, needing to be fixed, needing to change? Was I telling the story of how bad I had it so people would feel sorry for me? Were they mirroring back to me what I felt about myself, that I felt sorry for me too?

It wasn't the walking or not walking. It wasn't the walker, wheelchair, or the Muscular Dystrophy that was creating my suffering. It was the beliefs I had about walking or not walking, walker, and wheelchair. They were knocking me out of Alignment and keeping me from being open to all the gifts and possibilities that were always available to me but were hidden from view behind my glasses of lack.

By moving myself back into Alignment, I could hear the gentle calling to get a wheelchair, and by taking that action, I created a space for the true essence of who I am to rise up and flow in and around me.

My creativity began flourishing, and I began to grow and expand beyond anything I ever dreamed was possible as a woman walking. It was like giving birth to my true essence and a fresh start for a life being asked to be lived. I had reconnected with the woman I was born to be.

What I realized is that by focusing on wanting my reality to change, for it to be different than what it was, it hurt. It was depressing and sucked the energy out of me. But, if I instead moved into the Alignment Zone, I could perceive all that was happening as an experience. In that moment, I could choose to chill, lay back, glance out, and get my brain to start asking different questions. Instead of asking what am I losing, I could ask, what am I gaining? Instead of asking why is this happening to me, I could ask, how is this for me? Instead of asking what is being taken away from me, I could ask what gifts am I receiving?

So, when you say to me, "that's terrible that you have to go through that," or, "that must be awful being in a wheelchair," in my mind, I'm replying, "that's not my experience."

Like you, I believed that being in a wheelchair was the worst possible thing that could happen to me. It turned out to be the best possible thing that could happen to me because I discovered that my happiness had nothing to do with what was happening to me but everything to do with what was happening up in my mind.

I learned to listen deeply to what I was thinking, feeling, what emotions were rising, and how my body was reacting. I discovered that my natural state is peace, calm, and happiness, and the only thing keeping me from that are the limiting beliefs I am believing. All the time and energy I spent thinking about safety and what needed to change for me to be happy were now freed up. I was free, free for me, to do me.

A CONVERSATION

I would like to share a conversation I had with someone on social media about Alignment, pain, and illness.

Response: The problem with illness is the pain and suffering that usually comes with it, isn't it? There must be room for wanting to heal and accepting our illness as perfect at the same time.

Lori Brant: Loving illness is loving ourselves and everything in our experience. If taking medication or seeking treatment feels loving, then that too is loving, as long as I am not thinking my body should be doing something different in the moment... that is not loving. God is the medication, the treatment, the illness, and the pain. Our judgment that any of it is good or bad is not loving ourselves or God unconditionally and disconnects us from who we really are.

Response: It is very hard not to want your body to be something different when you are in pain or in a weakened body, though. I do not think I achieved that. Not many do. It must be enlightenment, and I mean that seriously.

Lori Brant: It is different than what we are trained to do. Yes. But, how awesome would it be if our "go-to thinking" was to focus on how amazing our bodies are? How amazing cancer is just to grow and grow. What if we could embrace the amazingness of that? What if we could only grow and grow spiritually like cancer?

What this different way of thinking does is create a state for health within us. A perfect state of wellness and support for our bodies to do what they do best - heal and regenerate.

We do ourselves and others a disservice when we believe our bodies are wrong, doing something they shouldn't be doing because it creates stress and resistance. I may have an illness, and the illness is going to do what the illness is going to do. I can stay aligned and love myself unconditionally, illness, and all, or I can disconnect, judge my body, my circumstances, and distance myself from who I really am. Which way is more conducive to happiness and wellness?

Response: Because I am a human being having a physical reality, I can clearly state that I do not prefer to be in pain.

Lori Brant: I hear you. When I catch myself preferring something different, I try to stay in Alignment and love the experience, find the gifts in having pain and not having pain. Then, I take Tylenol, lol, loving the whole experience, including the gift of Tylenol.

You can't love and fear something at the same time because fear takes you out of the moment. It is a belief that you don't want to lose what you have or won't get what you want.

Response: I do think you can love something and not desire it. :) That is different from fearing it.

Lori Brant: I think that I too still have preferences. I believe that having a preference is still seeing reality as good or bad. Therefore, it is judgment, and as a result, I am out of Alignment. But, if I honestly love each the same, (like chocolate vs. vanilla ice cream), then I really am just choosing from two examples of perfection (or ice cream) lol, I can stay in Alignment and choose.

Response: When I couldn't breathe well, a while ago, it didn't really feel like I was judging this as good or bad; it felt inherently undesirable. That's how I feel about pain as well. :)

(This next segment is the same story told earlier in the book, but I repeated it here because it was part of our conversation)

One day I lost my balance and fell, landing on the ceramic tiled floor. I was on my back, alone, with no idea how I would stand back up again. My old way of being would be to focus on the pain, start crying, and think thoughts like, "Why is this happening to me? Why me? I can't take this anymore." My preference would have been to be standing and not to have fallen.

In that moment, I asked with a little sarcasm, "What could possibly be the gift in this?"

As I was lying down on the kitchen floor, sensing my preference to want to stand, I opened myself to loving the experience entirely. I tried to find the gifts in falling. It took me a few minutes, but I noticed the ceiling, a different perspective of my home; I noticed that the cool ceramic tiles felt good on my back, I stretched out. I saw dirt on the kick plate of the cupboard and wiped it away. I kept doing this until I slowly got back in Alignment, moving from preference to choice, and calmly proceeded to try to stand.

That's one reason I believe there is a difference between loving something completely and preferring something to be different.

Response: I totally agree with your approach! The only caveat I would add is that if you were in acute pain from the fall, I honestly believe you would have felt differently. That's just part of our reality. :)

Lori Brant: There was pain and a big case of "What could possibly be the gift in this?" But this can be done regardless of the experience.

Response: When I prefer to have fish instead of scallops, does it imply that one is bad and the other good? To my mind having a preference among choices is simply choosing among items of (almost) equal "value".

Lori Brant: When one loves everything in their experience, the wanting for reality to be different no longer exists. What I mean by preference is that, when reality presents you with fish and scallops, you would be out of Alignment if you preferred chicken.

Response: I like the theory of what you are saying, Lori, but the reality is different as we are human and do not take well to pain. Only the truly enlightened do not mind and accept the lot.

Lori Brant: I am passionate about practical metaphysics. Nothing bugged me more than perfectly healthy people telling me to just change my thoughts and I'll feel better. What inspired me to find a better way was the true realization that everything, everything that exists is God and if everything is God then everything is perfect, no exceptions.

When I embraced that and looked for the gifts (God) in everything, (pain, illness, accidents, diagnosis, divorce, etc.), I felt good. When I felt good, I stayed in Alignment. When I stayed in Alignment, I was able to clean up my limiting beliefs and see solutions and possibilities that were blocked.

I am just proposing that it is a real possibility as a human to do it because I did it. This is not acceptance. It is unconditional love.

I always have a choice. I can be in pain and prefer something else or, I can be in pain and find/feel the gifts in the experience. One choice feels good and I stay in Alignment, and one feels bad and I get out of Alignment with who I really am. Regardless, in that moment, I am going to be in pain. My choice is how I want to move through it. It is possible to lovingly move through that which seems insurmountable. If I stay aligned while in pain, I am doing everything I can to create an unconditional loving space for my body, I'm keeping myself open and receptive to the next step, and I am growing and expanding. I understand that the pain is what needs to happen because it's happening. I'm not creating stress by trying to resist it, but instead, I'm allowing the pain to come and allowing the pain to go.

If I want or desire healing, I move out of Alignment which creates suffering on top of the pain. I'm creating more pain.

Is this process challenging? For me, yes, it is. Doable? In my experience, yes, it is. Am I able to do it all the time? No.

What is more important to me now is not, whether or not I am in pain but whether or not I am in the Alignment Zone.

Solutions or Problems

The more I work with limiting beliefs, the more I recognize that problems are only perceptions of neutral experiences. I have found that every problem can be perceived just as easily as a solution by entertaining a different perception of an experience.

It is our mind that has the habit of judging the moment as bad or good and it is the mind that can be directed to see the solutions rather than the problems. We just need to redirect our attention from the mind to become aware if we are in Alignment or not.

What if for every perceived problem, we entertained a different perception by seeing it as the solution? What if we trusted that there were no problems, but only a perception that made it so?

Let's say, for example, my car breaks down. If I choose to see it as a problem, something that is wrong, something that should not have happened, that perception draws me out of Alignment, triggers negative emotions while I try to find a solution. My solution may be to call a tow truck.

Now, let's say that my car breaks down, and I choose to see it as an experience. It's neither good nor bad, just an experience I'm having with my car. I stay in Alignment by not judging it as good or bad and keep myself open to my next step forward. In this case, it appears to be to call for a tow truck.

The solution, then, is the next action that I'd take. Instead of following through with the habit of seeing the situation as a problem and finding a solution, we can trust that there is no problem in every moment and, therefore, no need for a solution. There is only the next action to take. We don't have to move out of Alignment to know what the next action to take is.

Having a problem is an option.

It is only a limiting belief that makes us believe there is a problem. Perceiving problems draws our Awareness outward, and perceiving solutions draws us back inward. By questioning our limiting beliefs, we can create a new habit, where we automatically see the solutions before the problem arises and understand that moving out of Alignment is not required.

If we begin seeing reality as an experience rather than a series of problems or challenges, we can remain in the Alignment Zone, enjoy our experiences and remain open to an infinite number of possible, next, best actions that we can take.

Acceptance Is Not A High Enough Standard

People told me that I needed time to process my loss. People told me I needed time so I could learn to accept my situation.

Learn to accept my situation? That sounded like a pretty low standard to live by. It's like stating, "My life sucks, but I'm OK with it." Really? Is that the expectation I wanted for myself? Instead of my life sucks, I'll rise to the state of, "suck it up?"

Acceptance to me was synonymous with tolerance and if I was tolerating my life, I was not loving my life, and if I was not loving my life, I was never going to feel the happiness my heart longed for. Acceptance was a false state of Alignment and it was keeping me in the Outside Zone.

I invite all of us to raise the expectation of what's possible and question the thoughts that are preventing us from connecting more deeply with our natural state of peace, calm, and happiness. It's time to set a new standard, set a new expectation of what is possible in the moment. It's time to stop delaying the happiness that exists right now. It's time to require more of ourselves so that we can experience what is our divine right. We need only one standard, Alignment, so we can see the possibilities, notice the beauty, and recognize that we require nothing outside of ourselves. We need to see ourselves as a gift, to witness the beauty of our existence, and acknowledge that we already are what we are looking for.

Chapter 6

DRAWING OURSELVES BACK INTO THE ALIGNMENT ZONE

An Alternate Thought

When people looked at me using a walker or a wheelchair, I imagined what they thought. "What's wrong with her?" It was like thought bubbles popping out around people's heads that would say, "I'd hate to be in a wheelchair. That would suck. Look how skinny her legs are."

When I perceived people projecting those judgments, they landed hard, but it only happened if I moved out of the Alignment Zone. I needed to believe I was broken and not enough, to feel the brokenness and not-enoughness. If I were in alignment, I would know I was whole and complete just as I was, and brokenness would have nowhere to land. Those thoughts, I am broken, I am not enough would just pass through. You may see me as broken. I can understand where your perception of brokenness comes from, but the thought, "I am broken," would just be that, a thought. When I am in the Alignment Zone, the thought, "I am broken," would pass into my experience and out of my experience, and would have no negative emotional charge.

If I did notice an emotional charge or discomfort within my body, that would indicate to me that I have attached to the limiting belief and have moved out of the Alignment Zone. It would suggest that somewhere within me, I believed the thought, "I am broken," and would no longer be seeing, feeling, experiencing the magnificence of who I really was. Instead, I would be seeing, feeling, experiencing myself as separate from that.

I cannot be aligned and believe I am broken at the same time. I cannot be in the Alignment Zone and believe I am not enough. It's the "believing" in a limiting belief that obscures the truth of who I am.

The thought, "I am broken" can be experienced in the Alignment Zone as a thought. They can exist simultaneously. Lots of thoughts pass in and out while I am aligned with my true self. It's when I attach to a thought by believing it's true, that the essence of who I really am becomes blurred. The thought I attach to takes the stage front and center of my mind demands attention, and blocks the true essence of who I am, noticeable by the discomfort it creates.

I am not powerless in this process. I can interrupt the process by intentionally instructing my brain to consider focusing on an alternate thought. A thought that is more aligned with my true nature and a thought that will help me move back into the Alignment Zone before I move too far out. Instead of attaching to the thought "I am broken," I can attach to the thought, "I am whole and complete just as I am."

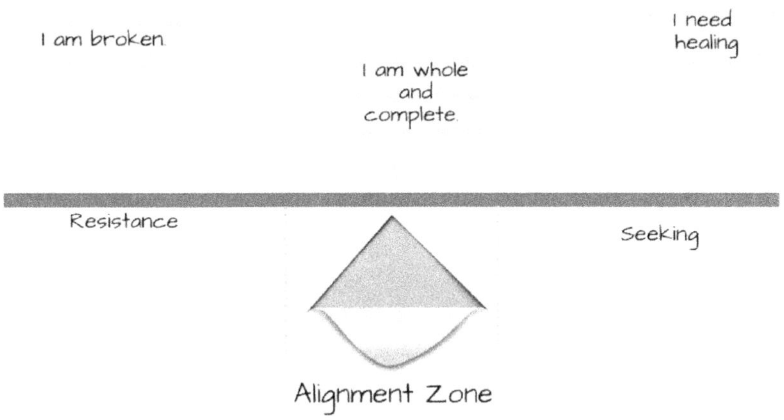

I can intentionally direct the mind to search for examples in my life of how "I am whole and complete," until I can shift myself back into the Alignment Zone.

Suppose I cannot come up with solid, empowering examples of how I am whole and complete. In that case, I may have to find a thought that is more closely related to the negative belief but more positive than the original negative thought. Initially, "I am fixable, or some parts of me are not broken," may be more believable by the mind than "I am whole and complete."

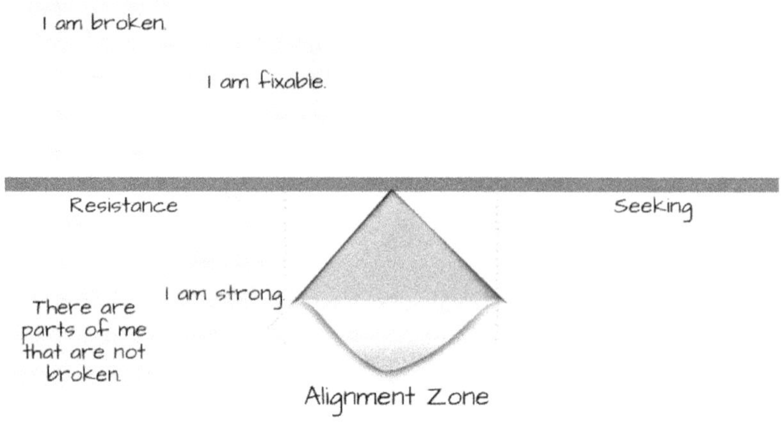

It's easier when I am triggered to find examples of how, "Some parts of me are not broken," rather than find examples of how "I am whole and complete." As long as I am moving towards the Alignment Zone, I am intentionally changing my experience.

Try it. Think the thought I am broken. Watch how your mind searches for examples of how you are broken. Notice how it feels in your body.

Now, think the thought, "There are parts of me that are not broken." Watch how your mind searches for examples of wholeness or parts of you that are whole. Notice how that feels in your body.

If you're like me, the second thought felt different. My body felt lighter inside, like a heaviness lifted. Not entirely, but there was a change. I was changing the experience I was having by changing the thoughts I was thinking.

We can live our days in The Alignment Zone with more peace and calm by recognizing when we are not aligned and taking measures to draw ourselves back into alignment.

Being Aware When You Are Moving Out of Alignment

Using a wheelchair amongst people who don't, has required me to dig deep, so I don't waiver from my truth and understanding that at any given moment, I am perfect just the way I am.

I was at this trade show as a vendor and had a table in a room full of amazing, loving, beautiful, and influential practitioners. Each specialized in a technique or strategy that helped others to recognize who they really were and to live life from that understanding.

Throughout the day, I was approached by the other practitioners, each with their own unique twist on how they believed they were the perfect person to help heal me. They also made judgments, disguised as compliments about how wonderful it was that I was there in my wheelchair.

"It's great that you are here with us, still doing spiritual work."

"I think it is so brave of you to have a table at the show."

"You seem happy. Wow, that's great that you can still find happiness."

"Are you able to take care of yourself? Do you have other people that can love and support you?"

I listened. I thanked them and then sat quietly, affirming silently in my mind that I was the divine plan in action, perfect, just as I was. That even though I used a wheelchair, I was just as unique, loving, beautiful, and powerful as they were because I existed. I affirmed that although we may appear different on the outside, we are all the same on the inside. I was using a positive stream of thoughts or a mantra to keep myself in the Alignment Zone.

But there was this one particular vendor who leaned in kindly and said, "I know a doctor that cured muscular dystrophy. You should look him up. He's cured everything, including DNA abnormalities."

I knew he wanted to help me. I knew he had good intentions, but I also knew he saw me as less than, unhealthy, and needing to change.

It did not matter what he thought, though. It only mattered if I was in the Alignment Zone. If I remained aligned with my true self, I would physically feel peaceful, calm, and loving, which would maximize my body's health. My verbal response from a state of peace and calm would be loving too. I'd say something like, "Thank you."

But that's not what I did. I was out of alignment. I had attached to the stream of negative thoughts and entered resistance. I was fed up, tired of everyone seeing me as broken, wrong, and needing to be different. I was tired of working so hard to stay in alignment because of what other people did or said. I resisted his help and his suggestion, evident by my response.

I defensively replied, "Thank you for letting me know, but I believe I am the divine plan in action, perfect in its design, and that although I may appear different, I have been created by the same loving source. We are all masterfully crafted, as a unique expression of love, full of talents and skills."

He replied, "That may be so, but what if you are not supposed to be in a wheelchair and are supposed to be walking like the rest of us? If you were healed, you would be more able to share your gifts with the world."

I could feel the desire to be healed rise up. I could feel the shift into more profound resistance. My heart sank. I started to attach to more negative thoughts. They grew in strength and numbers as my mind began building a case of how I was not OK the way I was. "What if I was wrong? What if I am supposed to try to be different? If I were like them, I'd be able to contribute more, be greater than I am now. I'm not good enough the way I am. What must they think of me? What are they saying about me? What if I can't keep up with them. What if it doesn't matter what I do? I'll never be like them. I need to be like them. I did this! It's my fault. I need someone to heal me."

All of that, BAM. It all happened in a split second. I had started to believe that it was wrong for me to be me and that I needed to change. My Awareness shifted from being aligned with my inner wisdom, my true self in the Alignment Zone, to the resistance of what is, to the mind's judgments, comparisons, and outside circumstances. More and more thoughts moved in. I need more, need to do more, need to be more. I'm not this enough or that enough. I'm not educated enough, successful enough, healthy enough, don't give enough, or love enough. I was spiraling.

Half listening as he continued to elaborate about the guy he knew, I noticed the physical sensation of being drawn outwards, away from my true self. I noticed my energy change. I noticed that I went from feeling love, connection, peace, and calm to a feeling of discomfort, agitation, and emptiness.

So many times, I have empowered my thoughts of lack by allowing my mind to take off, unchecked or verified, and allowing it to create truths where none existed. So many times, I have bought into stories or the perceptions of lack and allowed them to permeate my experience, drawing me away from my inner connection with my true self. So many times, my Awareness has been pulled outward, allowing one thought to attach to an army of thoughts, creating a war of judgment, comparison, and leaving me feeling diminished and fearful.

I chose in that moment to not resist my greatness any longer. I chose to stand in my truth, stay aligned with my true self, with who I really am. I chose to remain in my natural state of peace, calm, and happiness. I chose to stay in the Alignment Zone.

And so, in that moment, I gently drew my Awareness inward, detached from the mind's stream of thought, and began affirming silently that I was unique, loving, beautiful, and powerful just as I was. I sought proof, real-life examples of how each affirmation could be true, and I noticed that with each example, I shifted closer to the Alignment Zone until finally, I physically sensed peace and calm embrace me. Once I was back in the Alignment Zone, I looked at that prominent, beautiful practitioner and said, "Thank you. I'll consider looking into it."

I am responsible for how I feel, think, react, and respond. I am either feeling, thinking, reacting, and responding from a state of inward alignment with my true self, as Awareness, present, and in a state of peace, calm, and joy, in the Alignment Zone. Or, I am feeling, thinking, reacting, and responding from the unverified thoughts of the mind, gathered, organized, supported with biased evidence, and emotional ties with the sole desire to keep my Awareness focused anywhere but inward, in the Outside Zone.

I am Awareness. You are Awareness. That is the true essence of who we are.

As Awareness, we can observe our experience. We can become aware of our body, how it feels, how it is reacting. We can be mindful of our emotions, and we can observe or be aware of our thoughts.

When we, as Awareness, feel, think, perceive, react, and respond from the Alignment Zone, mentally, emotionally, and physically it feels like peace, calm, and joy. We're just enjoying the show.

When we, as Awareness, feel, think, perceive, react and respond from the limited beliefs or perceptions of the mind, mentally, emotionally, and physically it feels like discomfort, agitation, anger, sadness, or stress. We're in the show.

When I got agitated by the vendors at the trade show seeing me as sick and needing to change, I was still Awareness, but I was no longer aligned with it. It's like I lost the ability to observe and instead jumped into character like an actor in a movie, believing, behaving, feeling, thinking like the character. I fell into the story of how I needed to change and how I was not good enough the way I was. The story seemed so real that I lost touch with the true essence of who I was. My mind was not aligned with my heart.

But because my natural state is Awareness, I can either watch the show or be in the show. At any time, I can bring myself home or let myself play out the drama of my mind. Either way, peace, and calm are available to me. Alignment is always available to me. By tuning in to my body, I can recognize the physical sensations of discomfort when I am out of the Alignment Zone. I can choose to draw my attention, or my focus, inward, and transform my experience.

There Is Always an Alternative Way of Looking at Things

There is this strange behavior that arises that still catches me off guard. Being a wheelchair user often makes me stand out in a crowd, and I get that. I catch myself looking at others who use a cane, have a cast or walker. You know, looking but trying to look like you are not looking. I don't think I am nosy. I am just really curious. It's kind of like the curiosity you'd have if you saw a rock star or famous actor. You just gotta look.

I was standing in line with a friend, waiting at a funeral home to pay my respects, when the gentleman in front of me turned around and asked, "Can I sit on your lap?"

Really? At first, I could feel myself wanting to give him the look. The "You are weird," look. Then, I took a breath and acknowledged that it's just his reaction to something different; he's awkward because he feels uncomfortable with me in a wheelchair.

You might be thinking, no, that's not it, he's just being friendly. Maybe you're right, but this is not the first time this has ever happened. I have had this request many times, but I still can't seem to get used to it. Let me ask you, how many times have people asked you to sit on your lap in the spirit of being friendly? I guess if I was at a bar, I might be flattered, but I was slow to respond given the circumstances.

"If you must," I replied. I certainly wouldn't stop someone from plopping down on my lap if that was really what they needed. If they were about to faint or pass out or something, but in this situation, that didn't seem to be the case.

My response appeared to satisfy him until about 10 minutes later when he turned back around and asked, "Can I sit on your lap now?"

I am not sure I would ever ask to sit on a stranger's lap. Maybe if Johnny Depp was behind me, I might ask, but even that might be a stretch. I mean, what do you say to that request? "Sure, that would be wonderful?" Or do I say, "No?" That sounds like I am rude. Whatever response I give to that type of request never seems appropriate.

I may use a wheelchair, but I don't feel or do anything differently than anyone else. It's like wearing a pair of comfortable shoes. You use them to get around comfortably. In the rest of my life, I shower, get dressed, eat, drink coffee, go to work, watch T.V., swim, spend time with family. The wheelchair is not really on my radar 24/7. Famous people, too, live very regular lives. They get dressed and eat breakfast just like the rest of us, but they stand out when they are out in public or performing.

Being in a wheelchair is kind of like being famous. I'm doing the same thing as them. They are just regular people having a unique experience that makes them appear different, and therefore people act differently around them.

So.... I am living the life of a rock star!

I've got strangers propositioning me in public; I get reserved parking, dedicated entrances, I go to the front of the line at amusement parks and concerts.

This whole time I was thinking they were feeling sorry for me. I have so many more privileges than the average person.

I board planes first, have dedicated washrooms everywhere I go. People open doors for me; I have special entrances. People carry my bags. I get special seating. I never have to worry about reserving a seat; I have one, specifically designed for my comfort, everywhere I go.

That guy in front of me, the one who asked to sit on my lap, was just pointing out the obvious. He wanted to be like me and have the privilege to sit down in line too.

Isn't that amazing. I just opened myself up to a new perspective. Nothing outside of me changed, but how I saw the outside had changed.

This makes me think that maybe I should take a look at the rest of my life and see where else I'm judging people and life, seeing things only one way, one perspective of how things are. Maybe, things are good or even better than I thought. I just have to open myself up to it and entertain a new perspective.

I can't wait. I'm gonna have a blast riding around, smiling at my adoring fans, and enjoying the special treatment.

Next time when a stranger asks to sit in my lap, I think I might just say, "Yes," and I'll be sure to have a pen handy just in case they want my autograph.

Bull's Eye

When I refer to the Alignment Zone, I am referring to the state of being that is void of stress or suffering and where you feel joy, peace, calm, and happiness. The closer you are to the center of the Alignment Zone, the more aligned you become with your pure natural state, and the more peace and calm you'll experience.

It's not an all or nothing thing.

Just when I thought I experienced complete alignment, I would have a new experience of being aligned that would seem even more peaceful and calm than I had ever experienced before. Although I believed I had been previously aligned and not stressed, a form of discomfort would lift during the new experience showing me otherwise and would reveal to me more of my true self. This has been my experience for years. I have experienced more alignment with my true self in some moments versus other moments. When I experience these moments of deeper alignment, I experience a more profound love for myself, others, and the experiences I am having.

I don't know what complete alignment is, whether I have ever experienced it or if I ever will. If complete alignment is possible as a human being, I believe it would be experienced when one was void of all limiting beliefs because limiting beliefs are the only thing blocking the true essence of who we are.

However, if you set the goal for yourself to be in perfect alignment, you may actually push yourself further away from it because the seeking of anything draws you outward. Consider instead, bringing Awareness to the beliefs that are keeping you from a deeper state of alignment in the moment and transforming them.

It's like a dartboard. You don't have to hit the board in the red center circle with your dart to get points. You can land anywhere near and around the center to add to your score. The same goes for alignment. You don't have to be perfectly aligned to benefit from moving inward because, with each inward movement towards the center, you'll release stress and experience more peace and calm. You don't need a bull's eye or be perfectly aligned to make it count. Eventually, you end up experiencing a deep sense of alignment more often than you do now. You have briefer encounters with stress, and it becomes easier and easier to recognize when you're moving in and out of alignment.

Many people are embarrassed for being emotional, triggered, or experiencing negative thoughts, but it's a crucial part of our experience. Otherwise, you wouldn't be experiencing it. We all have a unique journey back to recognizing who we are, and those journeys can be all over the map. From the rapist to the raped, the bully to the bullied, the rich to the poor, or the athlete to the physically challenged. We are all beautiful, unique expressions of God. What appears to be our life is God experiencing itself through a physical body. The essence of all that we are is God. Reality is God expressed. The only thing keeping us from being aligned and living from that understanding is our limiting beliefs, and any movement back to experiencing that understanding brings you closer to a deep, all-encompassing love.

The Law of Attraction

The Law of Attraction believes that positive or negative thoughts bring positive or negative experiences into a person's life. By changing your thoughts, you can improve or alter different aspects of your life.

I was led to believe that if I changed my thoughts, I would change my physical reality. If I wanted a red sports car, I could change my thoughts, and poof, I'd have a red sports car in my driveway. If I wanted a body that did handstands, I could just change my thoughts, and poof, I'd be doing handstands.

It's my understanding now that I create my reality by the perceptions I have about it. If I perceive my experience as something good that resulted from my thoughts, my brain might say, "Look what I manifested. I created physical reality because of my positive thoughts. I manifested goodness." If I perceive my experience as bad, my brain might say, "Look what I manifested because I had negative thoughts. I manifested badness, or I created dis-ease."

The perception that I created reality by the thoughts I was thinking was formed by my mind's interpretation and judgment of reality.

Reality is the divine plan unfolding. It is what exists before my mind judges it as good or bad and before I assign responsibility. My thoughts about the divine plan unfolding create my unique perception of it. That's how I create my reality.

I can align myself and be open to the perfection of the divine plan as it unfolds, or I can remain in the Outside Zone, where the mind creates the illusion that I need to take ownership of it and need to control it.

When I am aligned, I am open. I see the gifts in having a car, and I see the gifts in not having a car. I don't need a new car, I'm just open to the information that a car can exist and not exist in my reality.

If I choose to focus on red sports cars, my mind will filter the information it gets from the divine plan unfolding related to a new car. I may start zeroing in on details about how much it costs, what could be done to obtain that money, opportunities to earn money, and begin to notice red sports cars when I am out and about. Not because they are suddenly appearing but because my mind is looking for them. I'm not creating red sports cars, they were always there, but my mind is focused and able to notice them now. This may potentially lead me to get a red sports car. If that happens, I might think I manifested it. That, **it was my thinking that manifested the red sports car** or the actions I took that brought the red sports car into my experience. I got the car because I controlled the unfoldment of the divine plan.

Is it not possible that the thought within me to get a red sports car was part of the divine plan unfolding too? That the information, outside circumstances, and the actions I took were all divinely orchestrated. My experience of that part of the divine plan was determined by whether or not I was in alignment.

Alternatively, if I have the thought that I want a new red sports car and I didn't get a red sports car, I might think I am not manifesting properly. That, **it was my thinking that prevented me from manifesting the red sports car,** and I am responsible for not controlling the unfoldment of the divine plan. Is it possible that the divine plan was unfolding and it did not include a red sports car? How I experienced that part of the divine plan was determined by whether or not I was in alignment.

Let's look at this from a third perspective.

Let's say that while in alignment, I have the experience of having a red sports car. **Wow, cool. I must need that.** Alternatively, while in alignment, I have the experience of not having a red sports car. **Wow, cool, I didn't need it.** I observe and enjoy the divine plan's unfoldment, trusting that God knows what he is doing and I don't need to control it. Everything is taken care of, including me.

Instead of focusing on acquiring a red sports car, in alignment, my thoughts and actions are drawn towards doing things that are aligned with the divine plan moment to moment. It might be to take action to get a red sports car or not, but either way, I know I will have exactly what I need and want because in alignment I want, what I have. I don't need anything outside of me, including a red sports car, to be happy. I experience happiness when I am on the same page as the divine plan.

If I am out of alignment in the Outside Zone and try to use the Law of Attraction to feel good, I am trying to change how I feel by manipulating outside circumstances to elicit happiness inside me. It won't work.

The thought in the first example, "**It was my thinking that manifested the red sports car,**" actually moves me out of alignment because it is taking responsibility for the manifestation of it and creating a slightly "better than before," perception. The belief that there is more than what already exists and I am experiencing less than what is available creates discomfort. But because pleasure is more closely related to the true essence of who I really am, the discomfort of being out of alignment may be undetectable in the moment.

In the second example, the thought, "**It was my thinking that prevented me from manifesting the red sports car,**" creates more discomfort because it connects easily to other limiting beliefs such as, "I can't do anything right. It doesn't matter what I do. I'll never get this. I am doing something wrong." These connections move me further out of alignment than the first example.

The thoughts, "**Wow, cool. I must I need that,**" and "**Wow, cool I didn't need it,**" keep me aligned.

Do you see the difference? In the third example, the divine plan unfolds, and I am the observer of what is, grateful that what I need is always provided. I don't need anything outside of myself because I always have everything I need.

If everything is universal source energy (God), everything is perfect just as it is. To say illness is less than, wrong, bad or should be cured is to say, God is less than, wrong, bad, and should be cured. An illness is just as much God or love as health is. Illness is a judgment of an experience, just as health is. Love or God is what exists as an experience before that same experience is judged as either bad or good by the mind.

Our journey here on earth is to align our head and heart so we can love ourselves and others completely, just as we are, just as they are, and by doing so, we are loving unconditionally, in perfect alignment with God.

I have heard over and over again, "You Create Your Own Reality." Especially from those who seem to have achieved or acquired what they wanted. But did they create their reality, or did what they want, match the reality that unfolded?

The Universe

I'm not sure who said it first, but I have heard references like, "We are not living, but are being lived," or "We are not doing, but are being done," and I struggled with the understanding of that. I had a hard time grasping what that would look like when it was applied to everyday life.

Both statements seem to suggest that we are not in control. It's hard to believe that we are not making choices, manifesting, or making things happen.

It got me thinking that it would be similar to the idea of a self-driving car. Imagine for a second that the Universe was a self-driving car. It drives on its own, knows where to go, and keeps us safe. It gets us where we need to be, on time, perfectly, moment to moment, lovingly supporting us, always. That's the divine plan unfolding. Perfectly designed and requiring no assistance from us, at all, ever. All we have to do is trust the loving Universe and sit back and enjoy the ride. This is our natural state. To just sit back and notice, moment to moment, the loving perfection of the Universe.

But we don't do that. We grab the wheel and try to control that which can't be controlled. We BELIEVE that we are the ones driving the car. We BELIEVE we choose what we do, where we go, and believe we are making the maneuvers that need to be made to keep us safe.

We've got a firm grip on the steering wheel, making it turn left, making it turn right. Sometimes we floor it, sometimes we coast. Sometimes we slam the breaks hard, refusing to budge. We genuinely believe that we are driving the car and are oblivious to the fact that our efforts are not required and have zero impact on our trip.

When our efforts to control our destination line up with the car's destination, we believe it was our efforts that got us there, and that reinforces our idea that we created our reality. When our efforts to control our destination do not line up with the car's destination, we think we did something wrong.

But all the while we're being driven, automatically, perfectly, lovingly to a predetermined destination.

Cleaning up our limiting beliefs and LES loops help us to release our grip on the steering wheel, opens us up to trusting the Universe and seeing the gifts in the moment. When we relinquish our illusionary control, we begin to see that our path is the perfect path. Our body is the perfect body. Our experience is the perfect experience because it is divinely orchestrated to bring us back to who we really are. It's freedom.

We are not the driver of the divine plan but are being driven by the divine plan. Our life is designed to be the perfect RIDE, and it's only our thoughts that can take us off course.

Chapter 7

HOW OLD STRATEGIES KEEP US STUCK

I'm So Distracted

"I'm so distracted. I need to be more accountable," my client said.

She was overwhelmed, and her calendar was so full that she never seemed to find the time to get to the projects she wanted to work on. Whenever anyone asked her to do something, she immediately said yes, without consideration of her already full calendar. She never contemplated if it was something she wanted to do or if it would take her away from completing personal projects. The busy-ness created a distraction.

I worked with her on her time management and developed new strategies that supported her efforts to complete her business tasks and personal projects. It worked for a bit, but it wasn't long before she found herself sitting down to work on her personal projects only to find new distractions. She went from keeping herself over the top busy as a distraction to using social media, household chores, or whatever else her mind could focus on distracting her from the personal project scheduled during that time.

The shift from one form of distraction to another told me that distraction was being used as a strategy. This client was using distraction to avoid feeling overwhelmed. Chances were, at some time in this client's life, she had felt a deep sense of being overwhelmed, and it scared her. It frightened her so much that she created a "distraction" strategy that helped her get relief from that feeling of being overwhelmed. People are often not aware that they have made such strategies to deal with negative emotions and are not aware that these strategies are continuously being played out in different aspects of their lives well into adulthood.

If I've had an experience that triggered negative emotions, my brain tries to find a way to alleviate the discomfort. The brain responds based on past results, experiences, or adherence to the already established belief system (LES Loop). If a response in the past provided relief from similar negative emotions, my brain would make the connection, "Hey that worked. Let's remember that and do it again the next time we feel overwhelmed."

For example, if I get criticized as a child for not being responsible, my brain may first create a limiting belief (I am not responsible). Next, the brain makes the connection between the limiting belief and how it felt emotionally and physically to be criticized as not being responsible (sadness, disappointment, heart sinking, sweating). Third, the brain searches the archives for a way to avoid those negative feelings or avoid situations where I would be put in a position of having to take responsibility. I might use strategies like letting other people lead, keeping myself small, not taking risks, or perhaps, avoid situations that put me at risk of having to be responsible. If I am not responsible for anything, then there is no risk of anyone expecting me to be responsible and less chance of feeling sad, embarrassed, or not good enough.

This may have seemed like a logical strategy to a child, but if left unmonitored, that strategy may continue to operate in my adult life and no longer provide the relief it was initially intended to deliver. Imagine the impact if, as an adult, I avoided taking responsibility for things.

My client's outdated strategy of using distraction to deal with being overwhelmed was not working for her. By volunteering for other people's projects and not working on her personal project to write a book, she ended up with a jam-packed calendar, with no free time to write. The outdated strategy she was using to avoid feeling overwhelmed was creating experiences that overwhelmed her. She was getting more of what she didn't want.

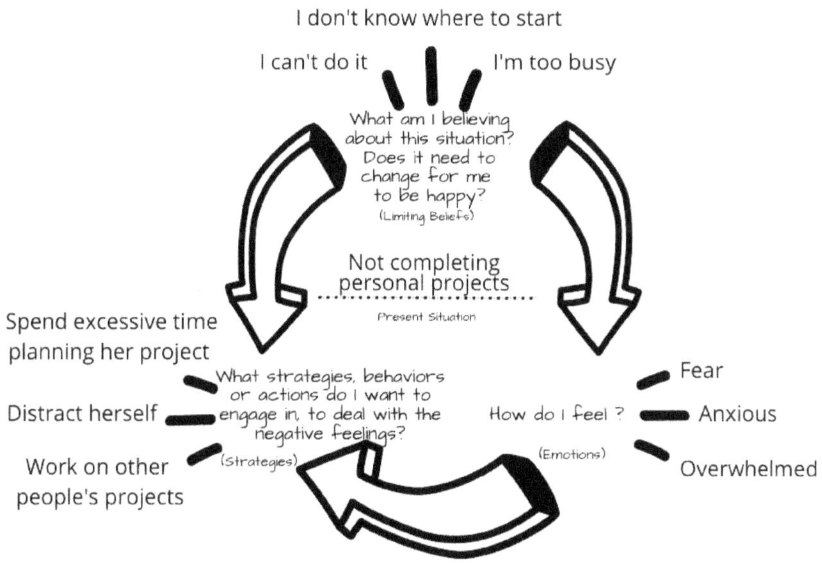

I had a follow-up session with this client. She reported that as soon as she decreased her busy-ness by scheduling time for personal projects, other distractions started popping up during personal project work time. She was recreating busy-ness. Then, the constant looping of thoughts about how she was not being productive or not being accountable during personal work periods made her feel overwhelmed. It was a no-win situation.

I asked my client, "What would you be afraid of if there were no more distractions and you completed your book?"

She replied, "nothing. It would be great. My book would be finished, I'd be super popular." Her smile disappeared, and shock set in, "I'd be in the limelight. But... I don't want the attention because people will judge me."

The client indicated it would be great and not great to complete the book. On the one hand, she would achieve her goal, and that would be satisfying. However, by completing her goal, she'd be thrown into the limelight and be judged. That's a limiting belief.

To be in the limelight is terrible. If I am successful, people will judge me.

So, I asked her, "Can you recall the earliest instance where you were in the limelight, and people judged you?"

Her jaw dropped, and she looked at me, "Yes, I was in grade 5, and my teacher asked me to go to the front of the room and demonstrate how to do a math problem on the board. I did it the way I thought was right, and suddenly, he just started yelling at me, telling me, I did it wrong, what was I thinking, how stupid of me."

I asked, "How did that make you feel?"

"Stupid, embarrassed, humiliated. I followed all the rules. I did what the teacher asked, and I didn't know any better. I couldn't trust myself to know what to do or what to do next."

"Did anyone judge you?" I asked.

"Yes. All the other kids and the teacher."

"You were in the limelight, doing what you thought you should do, to the best of your ability, and got punished for it. You got judged, and it made you feel stupid. Is that right?"

"Yes." Her shoulders dropped, and her head lowered. A gentle, teary release rose up and out of her. I watched as old emotion, maybe 30 years old, was finally being released, and a lightness washed over her.

Although this happened many years ago, the intensity of the experience and the emotions attached to it had been buried deep within the client. That's how limiting beliefs work. Her younger self perceived the classroom experience through the eyes and mindset of a grade five student, and this perception became a truth for her. Without questioning the belief as an adult, the view continued to be considered a fact, and her adult self, behaved in a way that avoided success and being in the limelight.

"Did you behave any differently, right after that incident, to avoid being in the limelight?

"I distracted myself." As she made the inner connection, a second emotional release, more profound than the first, eased out. "I would pretend I was writing or reading, whatever I could do to avoid eye contact so that I wouldn't get chosen."

"So, you wouldn't be in the limelight?"

"Yes."

She had created a LES Loop in grade 5 that was still influencing her life as an adult.

These are some of the Limiting Beliefs, Emotions, and Strategies that came up during that coaching session that keep the LES Loop active in her life.

Beliefs

It never ends.

It's better not to start.

It doesn't matter what I do.
It's too much.
The task is too big.
I don't know where to start.
I can't do it all.
I can't do it.
It needs to be perfect before I get started.
I can't trust myself to know what to do next.
I'm stupid.
I don't know what I am doing.
Circumstances need to be just right.
People will judge me.
I will let people down.
People will think I am fake.
I'm not supportive.
I'm not putting family first.
I'm not authentic.
To be in the limelight is bad.
People will judge me if I am successful.
I can't trust myself.
I need to do what people in authority ask me to do.
Only people in authority know how to do it.
I don't know what to do.

Emotions
Overwhelm
Frustrated
Tired
Fear
Stress
Shame
Stupid
Embarrassed
Humiliated

Unsure
Checked out
Small
Lethargic
Disappointed in self
Helpless
Fatigued
Disheartened
Off
Anxious

Strategies
Distract myself.
Say yes to other people's projects.
Keep busy.
Paralysis - check out.
Close down.
Keep the calendar full.
Busy-ness.
Cleaning/Social Media.
Making lists about what to do.
Not following through on scheduled personal tasks.
Work with others.
Keep small.
Don't stand out.
Avoid doing videos.
Avoid being in the limelight.
Don't start.
Restart from the beginning.
Spend a lot of time creating the plan.
Don't spend time on my own projects.
Don't complete personal projects.
Put myself down, negative self-talk.
Break down.

Check out.
Keep myself from being successful.
Keep myself from being in the limelight.

Strategies like distraction are used to keep oneself from feeling the negative emotion attached to a limiting belief. Once the strategy is identified, we can transform the limiting belief, the emotions attached to it, and the behaviors that are keeping them in place. We can begin to transform the automatic, habitual reactions by recognizing the connections between them. Through coaching, we created a strategic action plan of actions to change the LES Loop and support the client's ability to move through distractions, complete projects, and enjoy her successes.

People often come to coaching because they are stuck and they want to figure out how to be happy. The risk for new coaches is that they focus on what is wrong and what needs to be fixed instead of clarifying what a client wants. A new coach can easily be fooled to think that if they just work on time management, getting the client to focus more, eliminating distractions, using positive affirmations, setting goals, or setting positive intentions, the problem will be solved. But what if there is no problem? What if it is a LES Loop?

By clarifying what a client wants, where they are now, and listening deeply, I can hear the client's inner wisdom rising up and out of the conversation. I can hear what's not being said, what is being repeated, and uncover the motivation behind the behaviors that create unsatisfying results. By revealing that, my client and I can change the original cause of unsatisfying results and form decisive, powerful, positive actions that align with the client's goals.

My client contacted me a couple of weeks after her session and told me how identifying the LES Loop has had a tremendous impact on her life. She was now able to stay aligned in the Alignment Zone, accomplish tasks, and stay focused with new energy. She now records social media videos with ease, interacts with people differently, doesn't feel the need to prove herself by taking classes, and doesn't procrastinate. She even reported that the first draft of her book was almost finished. Everyday life was transforming before her eyes.

I Can't Think

Another client I had, used distraction as a way to dissipate fear and paralysis. When she misbehaved as a child, her mother would say, "Now you go out to that rock and sit and think about what you did." My client would go outside, sit on that rock, ponder her behavior, the consequences of what she did, and how she would proceed moving forward. She began associating the rock as being responsible for her decision making and knowing what to do next.

One day, she noticed that her dad was digging a garden in the back yard and ventured outside to watch. As she got closer, she realized that her father had inadvertently buried her thinking rock during the garden's construction. She was paralyzed. What would she do now that her rock was buried? How would she think? How would she know what to do? She wanted to express her fear to her father, tell him she needed the rock to think and make decisions but was scared that by criticizing his burying of the rock, she would risk being the brunt of his fury. So instead, she stood there and held her emotions inside. She was paralyzed. After standing there for what seemed to be an eternity, she went to her room and sat on her bed. She sat there until the feelings of fear and paralysis dissipated. In that moment, a new strategy was born to deal with her inability to think. She would use distraction to deal with the fear, hold back from expressing herself and wait until the paralysis dissipated.

As an adult, when she sat down to complete a project that required thought or decision making, fear rose up, and paralysis seeped in. The fear was an emotional response that, in turn, triggered her strategy of distraction. Frustrated with her inability to complete tasks, she often did household chores or activities that didn't require thinking until the fear disappeared.

Let's explore my client's LES Loop. First, there were **limiting beliefs**. In this case, the limiting beliefs were, "I don't know what to do. I don't know what to do next. I can't trust my thinking." Just to name a few. Those thoughts were connected to the little girl, standing paralyzed and scared when she realized the rock, responsible for her thinking and decision making, was now gone and buried.

Second, the limiting beliefs triggered the **emotions** or the fear that was attached to the memory of the buried rock. As an adult, fear now seeps in when she needs to think, speak, or make decisions.

Third, my client's brain needed a plan to get relief from the fear, so it searched for what worked in the past. It found distraction **strategies**, pushing down the unwanted feelings and ignoring them, not expressing herself, and sitting on her bed alone, waiting until the emotions shifted. Now, as an adult, rather than sitting on her bed, she engages in activities that don't require thinking, such as household chores.

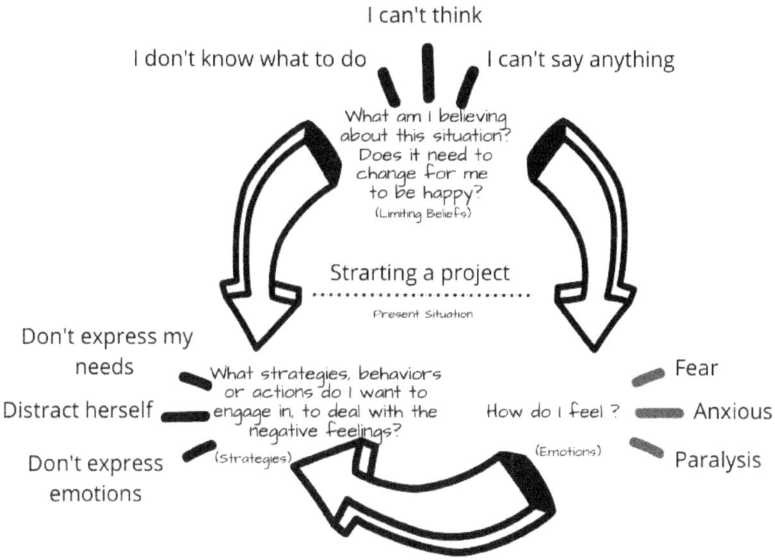

In addition, the strategies of distraction and not expressing herself triggered other limiting beliefs like, "I'm a failure, and I am useless," because she was unable to complete work projects. The LES Loop kept looping.

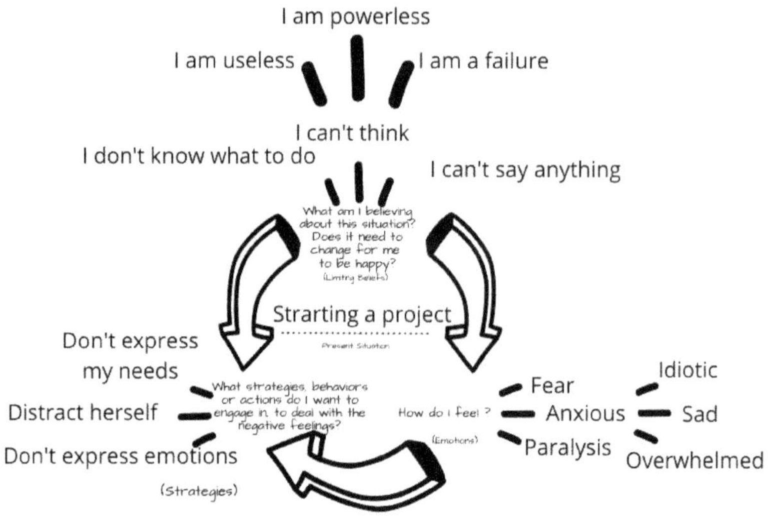

A limiting belief triggered an emotion, which triggered a strategy, which triggered a limiting belief, and so on.

Any action (strategy) launched in reaction to a triggered, narrowly focused mind is limited in its effectiveness because it feeds the LES (Limiting Belief/Emotion/Strategy) Loop instead of finding a new effective strategy to achieve a different result. That's why any action taken from lack creates more lack.

To make long-lasting change, the client needed to isolate the thought or thoughts that she believed to be true, identify what negative emotions they were connected to, and determine what strategies she had created to deal with them.

By recognizing, interrupting, and transforming the loop, my client and I could create new, life-affirming strategies to help her achieve her goals. Together, we could create a plan to break the client's habitual response of distracting herself while simultaneously developing a positive, supportive plan to move forward. That plan included learning how to use the Alignment Strategy to move back into the Alignment Zone when she had moved out.

Some of the Limiting Beliefs, Emotions, and Strategies that came up during our coaching session are listed below.

Beliefs
I can't think.
I'm not going to succeed.
I'm not going to be able to do it.
I am powerless.
I can't stand up for myself.
I can't think for myself.
I can't depend on people to follow through.
I'm a failure.
I am useless.
I am not good.
I am not authentic.
I am incompetent.
I am disruptive.
I can't do anything right.
I can't trust myself to think.
I am not going to get ahead.

Emotions
Overwhelmed
Fear
Afraid
Anxious
Awful
Sad
Mad
Idiotic
Paralysis

Strategy
Distract myself.
Be quiet.
Don't share my feelings.
Don't think.
Wait it out.
Be alone.
Walk around.
Eat.
Drink.
Don't speak up.

By moving into the Alignment Zone and being aware of her LES Loop, she changed her automatic, habitual reactions.

Mirroring

Some of us assign responsibility for our discomfort, sadness, or stress by selecting an incident, someone's behavior, or circumstances outside of us as the culprit.

I feel this way because....
...he won't change.
...she is moody.
...he is jealous.
...of my health challenge.
...I don't have enough money.
...I can't find my passion.
... it's snowing.

Assigning blame for a negative experience is a strategy people often use as part of old LES Loops. Blaming others is easier than transforming our LES Loops and having to change.

Why do we resist change? Change requires more effort. It's easier to keep doing what we've always done the way we have always done it. Let's face it. When things can be accomplished without much thought or effort, it takes less energy.

Another reason we resist change is that we're wired to find the path of least resistance. Our brains are wired to make connections, find similarities, form conclusions, and assimilate new behaviors into old patterns. If we're trying to create a new way of responding or developing a new behavior or habit, our mind will resist it. It will plead the case that the change we're attempting to accomplish is not working, not what we are supposed to do, and try to convince us to go back to the old way of doing things.

The third reason we resist change is that we're on automatic pilot. Change requires conscious awareness. That means we need to be paying attention by maintaining our state of awareness in the present moment to notice when we are reverting to old ways of being. When our automatic pilot gets turned on, we move through life without really recognizing the details of what we are doing. It is just like when we drive to the store, and when we get there, we realize we were not paying attention and can't remember how we got there.

Discomfort, sadness, lack, and stress are messages from the Universe, letting us know our awareness has strayed outward. Drawing our awareness inward, questioning what we believe, and transforming limiting beliefs are crucial to creating change.

The first step for inviting change is to stop blaming outside circumstances or people for our discomfort instead of expanding our perception by entertaining how our discomfort can be a gift. Discomfort can be a gift because it lets us know that our awareness has shifted outward and we are no longer aligned. Once aligned, we can question the thoughts we are believing and finally, transform them and the LES Loops they are connected to.

Mirroring can help us do that. **Mirroring is the projection of a personal limiting belief onto another person, place, thing, or experience.** It's a strategy used by the mind to avoid changing our LES Loops.

What that means is, **every time we see something as wrong or needing to change outside of us, that something is what needs to be worked on within us.** The projection is a neon sign or tool, informing us that a LES Loop is active.

I struggled with this one. It meant that everything I criticized, judged, compared, or saw as wrong in others indicated that I was critical, judgmental, or wrong and had moved out of the Alignment Zone.

For example, if I found myself criticizing someone as annoying or rude for butting in line at the grocery store, that meant that I had moved out of alignment, that I was believing a limiting belief, and that I was triggering a LES Loop within me. It was all me.

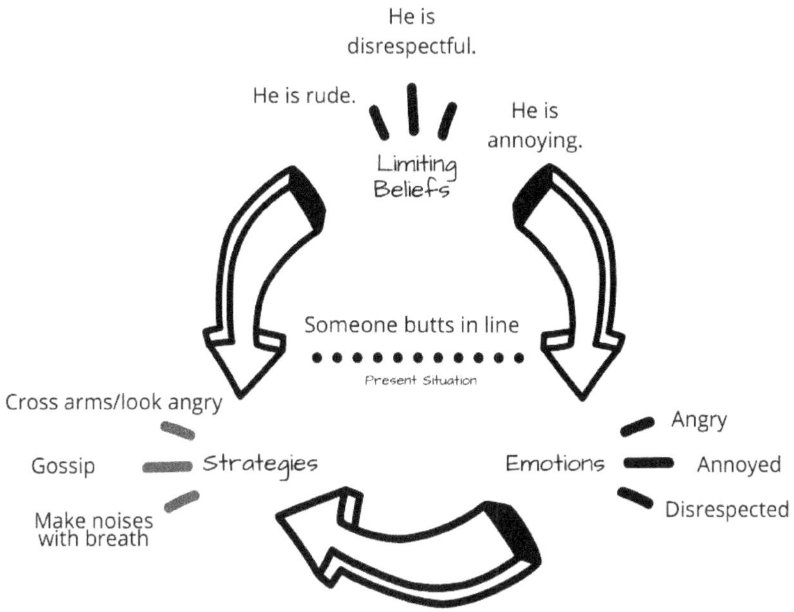

The first step in mirroring is figuring out how the outward projection can be turned around as an "I" statement. The simple way of doing that is finding the opposite of the projection. If I think he is rude, the "I" statement is, I am rude. If I think he is disrespectful, then the "I" Statement is, I am disrespectful. If, for example, I open myself up to experiences where I believed I was annoying, disrespectful, or rude, I can potentially break down and transform the LES Loop connected to it. By working on each belief individually, such as working with "He is annoying" I can ask myself, "Were there instances in my life when I was considered annoying?" Once I find those, I can complete the LES Loop by identifying the emotions and strategies attached to those instances.

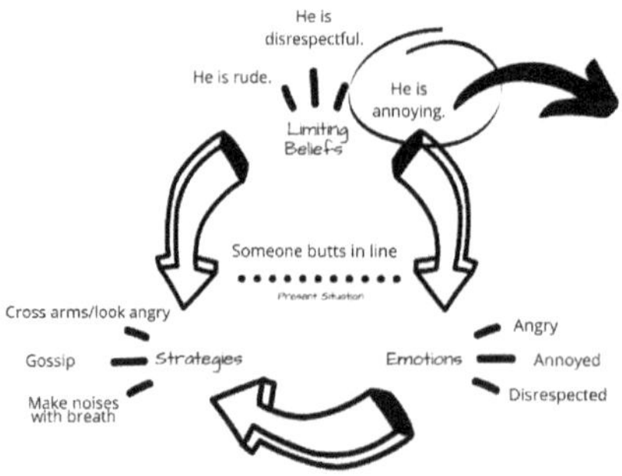

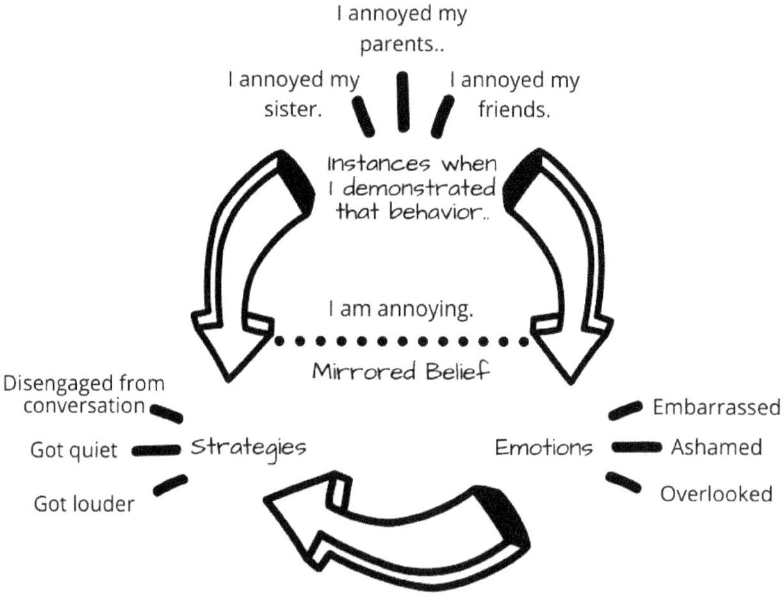

Here is an example of how mirroring can lead to uncovering LES Loops.

I had just moved into a new house, and the property was marked by steel rods indicating where the property lines were for my neighbor and me. One evening after dark, I observed my neighbor removing the rod from the ground between our two properties, but I didn't say anything. It seemed like each time I looked out my window, he was pruning the grass beyond the original property line and encroaching on my yard. I researched the laws for property surveys, the laws about removing markers, and requested the builder to re-establish the boundary. I told my brother and friends about my neighbors' deceptive behavior. I added stories about how he continually moved his man toys around in his driveway, including cars, a boat, and a jet ski. He was incredibly materialistic, and I was convinced he was taking advantage of me.

Imagine my surprise when the builder came to my door and informed me that my neighbor was pruning his own yard and he had not encroached. I was in fact, the one who was being materialistic.

My mind had taken in filtered information, interpreted it, and responded to the situation by criticizing and judging my neighbor as materialistic. He was mirroring back to me, what I needed to work on within myself. I was projecting my materialism onto him.

Let's take a look at the LES Loop.

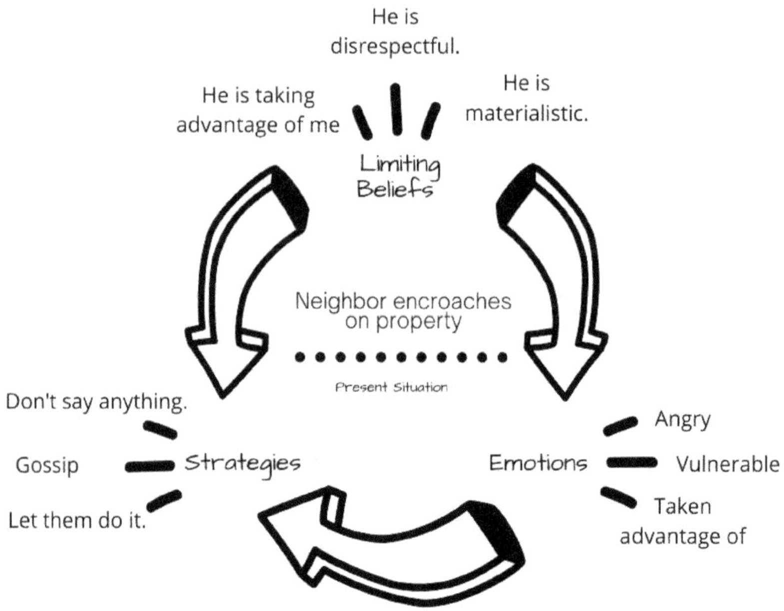

The limiting belief from the above LES Loop, "He is materialistic," can be converted into the mirrored "I" Statement, "I am materialistic." I could have chosen to work on the other limiting beliefs and their mirrored "I" Statements (I am disrespectful, I am taking advantage of him, I am taking advantage of me, I am encroaching on him, I am encroaching on me), as well. I chose "I am materialistic," because I felt the most significant, negative charge with that one. It would be helpful for me to use this process with all the "I" Statements, but I will only do the one "I" Statement here for demonstration purposes.

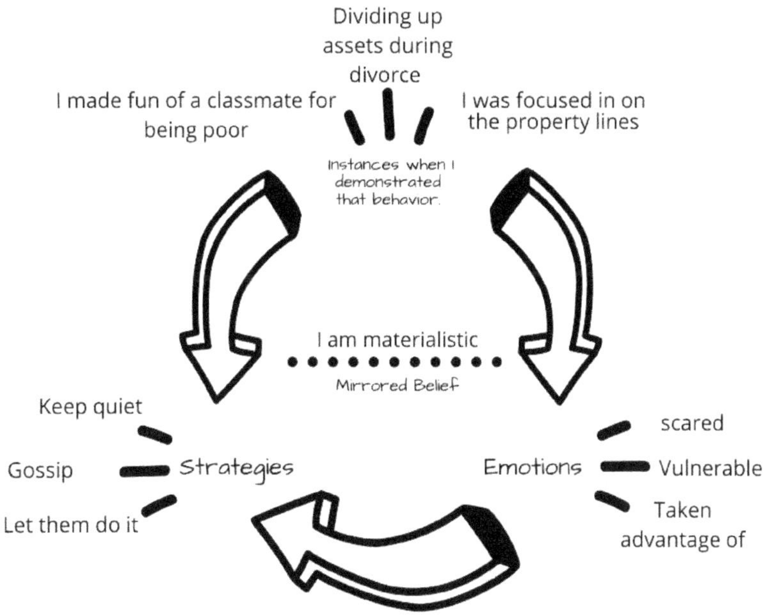

My anxiety had nothing to do with my neighbor or the property line.

My anxiety was triggered by the connection made in my mind with other limiting beliefs from my past and had nothing to do with my neighbor being **disrespectful** or **taking advantage of me,** which were the limiting beliefs from the previous, present situation LES Loop.

The memory of my divorce jumped out at me when I was completing the above loop, and I asked myself, "How was I materialistic during the divorce?"

I was materialistic because I was trying to hold onto as much money or household items as possible.

What did I believe would happen if I didn't have that money or household items?

I believed that:

- If I lose property, I lose money. (Materialistic)
- If I lose money, I am not safe. (Materialistic)
- I need to hold onto everything I own. (Materialistic)
- He is taking something I own away from me. (Materialistic)
- **He is taking advantage of me**.
- I am weak if someone **takes advantage of me**.

There is no place for me to record those beliefs on the loop, but I would note them while completing this process. By writing them down, I can observe and identify how everything is connected. On the surface, it seems absurd that my neighbor has anything to do with me being taken advantage of as a teenager. Still, by recording what comes up during the process, I can begin to see how materialism is linked to my divorce and is linked to being taken advantage of.

While contemplating those questions and their answers, another memory stirred within me. When I was younger, I had a boyfriend who **took advantage of me**.

For, "Instances when I demonstrated materialistic behavior," you'll notice that I only mentioned the instance of the divorce in the "I am materialistic," loop. Not the boyfriend. However, I always follow what comes up within me during the process rather than rigidly sticking to the template. The divorce, connected to the boyfriend's memory, and they both connected to being taken advantage of.

Therefore, it appears that the Limiting Belief, "I am being taken advantage of," is the common thread between the present situation with my neighbor, my divorce, and the boyfriend. In other words, the neighbor triggered my old LES Loop created when I was a teenager.

Through the mirroring process, I let go of the story with the neighbor and recognized that the emotions active within me were the emotions I experienced with the belief that I was taken advantage of. I took the first, earliest memory of when I believed I was being taken advantage of and completed the Earliest Memory LES Loop template. I used the earliest memory of the boyfriend because if I can transform that one, chances are all the other memories attached to it will be transformed as well.

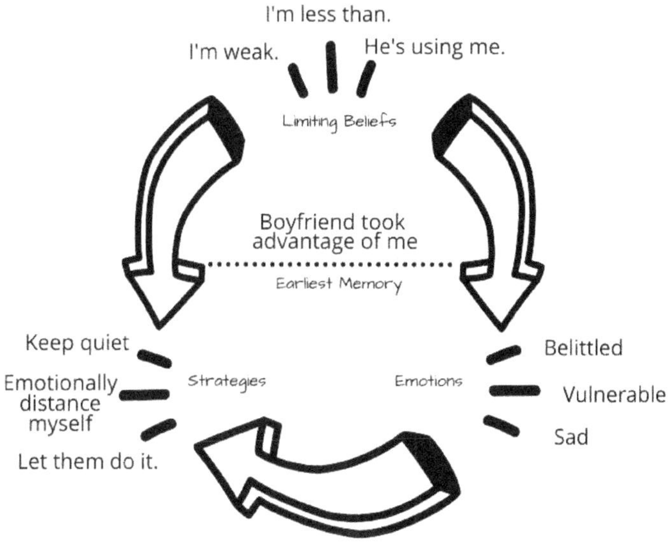

By looking at the three LES Loops, (Present Situation, Mirrored Belief, and Earliest Memory), you can see there are similarities, indicated by the circles below.

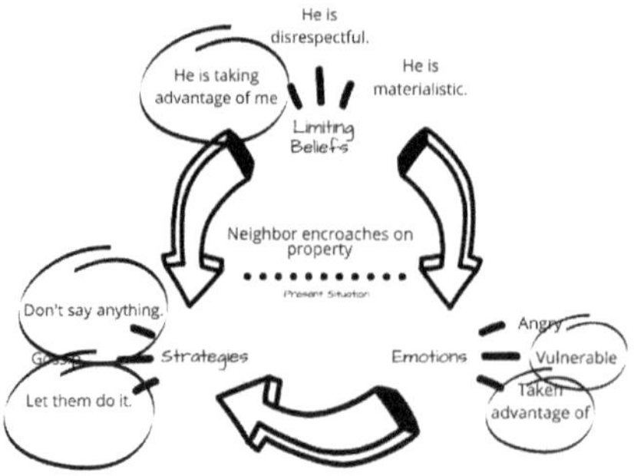

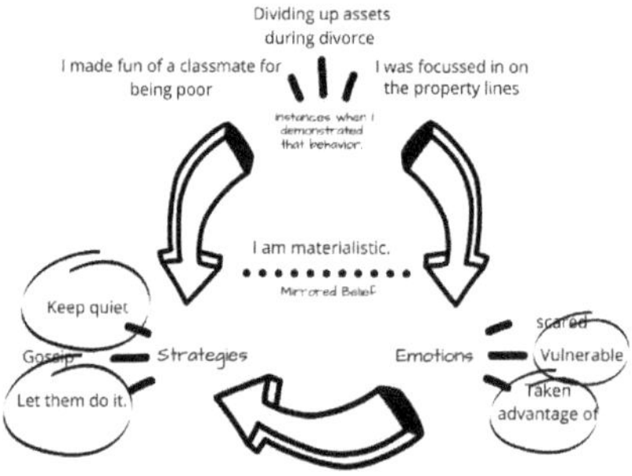

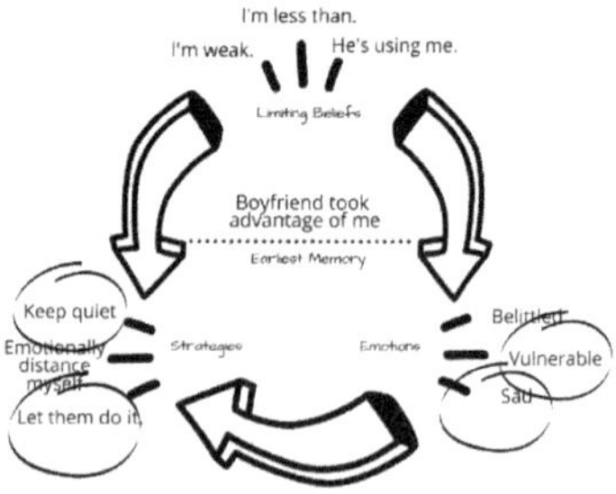

If I work on the Limiting Beliefs from my earliest memory of being taken advantage of, I can disrupt the LES Loop and bring choice as to how to respond. Instead of watching my neighbor pull out the stake and not saying anything, I can choose to go out and ask him to leave it in place because I am aware that to "stay quiet and let him do it," is an old, outdated strategy that no longer serves me.

I can then work on transforming the original Limiting Beliefs associated with the Earliest Memory Loop by aligning myself and asking, "Am I weak? Am I less than? Was I used?" Can I bring infinite perceptional awareness to those questions?

I am weak. When I sit with that in the Alignment Zone, knowing I am the divine plan unfolding, the answer gently rises within me, "no." I am powerful. I have moved through challenging experiences. I have confidently dealt with people who were strong, opinionated, and dominant.

I am less than. When I sit with that in the Alignment Zone, knowing I am the divine plan unfolding, the answer gently rises within me, "no." I am more than what I thought was possible. I am more than what others thought was possible, and I am loving life more than what was deemed possible.

He used me. When I sit with that in the Alignment Zone, knowing I am the divine plan unfolding the answer gently rises within me, "no." I used him to feel loved. I could have left. I could have said something. As far as he knew, I was OK with it. If I didn't say anything, how could he possibly know to stop?

When I am open to exploring the infinite perceptions that were available to me, I bring myself further into the Alignment Zone and begin to soften. I start to see that what I thought happened with that old boyfriend was only one of the thousands of perceptual possibilities of what happened. As a young girl, I chose one perception that created a negative emotional response, and I dealt with those feelings by developing a strategy of being quiet. I did the best I could given the tools and wherewithal at the time.

As an adult, I can choose differently. When I know I am feeling discomfort, I can choose to bring myself into alignment.

Emotional discomfort is always the result of an active limiting belief.

If I experience difficulty aligning myself, I can choose to ask the questions below or use the LES Loop templates to identify the cause of the discomfort.

-

Limiting Beliefs

What am I believing?

Why am I worried, scared, or angry?

What do I think I am losing?

How do I believe this will affect me?

-

Emotions

What am I feeling?

When have I felt this way before?

-

Strategies

What do I want to do in response to the situation?

Does that response resemble strategies I've used in the past?

My neighbor was just removing an obstacle. The story of how he was taking advantage of me, disrespecting me, and that he was materialistic was all in my head. I was projecting my story of how people take advantage of me onto him. My stress was created by me. I was creating my reality by having an unconscious LES Loop triggered within me and as a result, was filtering parts of the divine plan as it unfolded for evidence to keep it looping. My story, my reality, my experience. Basically, I was taking advantage of my neighbor by blaming him for my discomfort.

Finding The "I" Statement

One of the most challenging steps to identifying LES Loops is narrowing down the limiting beliefs to "I" Statements. Below is a chart of limiting beliefs discussed throughout the book and the questions I would ask during coaching sessions to draw out the limiting belief that keeps the client from being aligned. I encourage you to pick the "I" Statement with the biggest negative charge or the one you have the most resistance to.

It may be difficult to believe, but the negative thoughts we have about anything outside of us are thoughts we have about ourselves.

The negative thoughts we project onto others maintain our perception that we are less than what we really are. To align with our whole selves, we need to uncover and own those negative perceptions.

Belief	**Ask yourself these questions to zero in on "I" Statements**	**Mirrored Beliefs**
He is mean.		I am mean.
She is not doing enough.		I am not doing enough.
My car is broken.		I am broken.
It never ends.	What will happen to me if it never ends? If that happens, what does that say about me? Example: *I have no control. I am powerless.*	I never end. *I have no control.* *I am powerless*

It's better not to start.	Not starting will prevent what from happening? *Example:* *Things not working out as planned. Disappointment.* *If I started and things didn't work out as planned, what would that say about me?* *I'm a failure.* *It doesn't matter what I do.* *I'm stupid.*	*I didn't work out as planned.* *I am a disappointment.* *I'm a failure.* *It doesn't matter what I do.* *I'm stupid.*
It doesn't matter what I do.		I don't matter no matter what I do.
It's too much.	How does, it being too much, impact me? *Example:* *Overwhelmed, scared, depleted.*	I'm too much. *I am overwhelmed.* *I am scared.* *I am depleted.*
The task is too big.	How does, the task being too big, impact me? *Example: I don't know where to start.* *So, what does that say about me that I don't know where to start?* *I'm not smart enough.* *Overwhelmed.* *I can't do it. What does that say about me? I give up. I'm a failure.*	I'm too big. *I'm not smart enough.* *I am overwhelmed.* *I give up.* *I am a failure.*
I don't know where to start.	If I don't know where to start, what does that say about me?	I don't know where to start.

I can't do it all.	If I can't do it all, what does that say about me?	I can't do it all. I can't do it.
I can't do it.	If I can't do it, what does that say about me?	I can't do it.
It needs to be perfect before I get started.	If it is not perfect, what does that say about me? What might happen if it is not perfect before I get started?	I need to be perfect before I get started.
I can't trust myself to know what to do next.	What might happen if I don't know what to do next? What would that say about me if I didn't know what to do next?	I can't trust myself to know what to do next. I can't trust myself. I'm not trustworthy.
I'm stupid.		I'm stupid.
I don't know what I am doing.		I don't know what I am doing.
Circumstances need to be just right.	What might happen if the circumstances were not just right? What would that say about me if I went ahead and circumstances were not just right?	I need to be just right.
People will judge me.	What judgments would they make?	I judge people. I judge me.
I will let people down.	What might happen if I let people down? What would that say about me if I let people down?	I let people down. I let me down.

People will think I am fake.	What would that say about me, if people thought I was fake? What might happen if people thought I was fake?	I'm fake.
I'm not supportive.		I'm not supportive.
I'm not putting family first.	What would that say about me if I don't put family first? What would it say about me if I put me first?	I'm not putting me first. I'm not putting family first.
I'm not authentic.		I'm not authentic.
To be in the limelight is bad	What might happen if I put myself in the limelight? If that happened, what would people say about me?	I can't be in the limelight.
People will judge me if I am successful.	What judgments would people make about me if I was successful?	I judge people if they are successful. I judge people. I judge me.
I can't trust myself.		I can't trust myself. I'm not trustworthy.
I need to do what people in authority ask me to do.	What would happen if I didn't do what people in authority asked me to do? What does it say about me, if I don't do what people in authority ask me to do?	I'm not an authority. I'm not in authority.

Only people in authority know how to do it.	What might happen if I was not in authority and did it? If that happened, what would it say about me?	I'm not an authority.
I don't know what to do.	What might happen if I go ahead and do something without knowing exactly what to do?	I don't know what to do.
I can't think.		I can't think.
I'm not going to succeed.		I'm not successful.
I'm not going to be able to do it.	If I tried to do it and couldn't, what would that say about me?	I'm not going to be able to do it. *I am not good enough.*
I am powerless.		I am powerless.
I can't stand up for myself.	When I can't stand up for myself, that means I am ________.	I can't stand up for myself.
I can't depend on people to follow through.	What does that say about me when people don't follow through on the things, they said they'd do?	I can't depend on me to follow through. I don't follow through.
I'm a failure.		I'm a failure.
I can't do anything right.		I can't do anything right.
I am not going to get ahead.	If I don't get ahead, that means I am/I will __________?	I am not going to get ahead. I'm stuck.
I am disruptive.		I am disruptive.

The government is overreacting.		I overreact.
I spent all that money.	If I spent all that money, what does it say about me?	I spent all of me.
I need a vacation.	What will going on a vacation do for me? *Example: Relax. If I need to go on vacation to relax, what am I now? I am stressed.*	*I am stressed.*
Everything happens to me.		Everything happens to me.
I didn't need this right now.		I don't need this.
I needed the vacation to de-stress.		I'm stressed.
Not going on a vacation that has already been paid for, is a waste of money.	What does that say about me if I waste money?	I'm a waste. I waste money.
I needed a vacation for my mental health.	What might happen if I don't improve my mental health?	I'm not mentally healthy.
It needs to be perfect before I get started.	If it is not perfect, what does that say about me? What might happen if it is not perfect before I get started?	I need to be perfect before I get started. I need to be perfect.

I need her to call me.	If she calls you, what would that do for you? *Example: She cares. So, nobody cares until she calls you? If nobody cares, what does that say about you? I'm unloved. I don't matter.*	I don't care. I don't care about me. *I'm unloved.* *I don't matter.*
I need to know what to do.	If I knew what to do, that would mean I am __________? *Example: capable, I won't be hurt. I won't be wrong.*	I don't know what to do. *I am not capable.* *I am vulnerable.* *I am wrong.*
I need him to take the garbage out.	If he took the garbage out, what would that do for me? What message does that send if he takes the garbage out? *Example: He respects me.* *He loves me.* *I am supported.*	*I'm not respected.* *I'm not loved.* *I'm not supported.*
I need John's respect	If I had John's respect, what message would that send to me? *Example: He loves me. I'm valued.*	I'm not respected. *I am not loved.* *I am not valued.*
I need them to be quiet.		I am not quiet. I am loud.
They need to act their age.		I don't act my age.
I need his love.		I am not loved. I need my love.

I want a red sports car	What will having a red sports car do for me? *Example: I will be happy, free, have fun.*	*I'm not happy.* *I'm not free.* *I am not having fun.*
I want a new house.	What will having a new house do for me? *Example: I will be able to relax.* *If I am not relaxed, what am I?* *I won't have to worry about repairs.* *I'll have a bigger kitchen.* *So, if I had a bigger kitchen, what would that do for me?* *I'd have more space. I wouldn't be confined.*	*I am uptight.* *I am worried.* *I am confined.*
I want more money.	What would having more money do for me? *Example: I'd be free to buy what I want, wouldn't have to worry about bills. I Could buy a new car.* *So, if I had a new car, what would that do for me? What would having a new car say about me?* *I work hard and I deserve it. I am successful. Make me happy.*	I don't have enough money. *I am not free.* *I am worried.* *I don't work hard.* *I don't work hard enough.* *I am undeserving.* *I am not successful.* *I am unhappy.*

Relationships

I owe my Ex an apology. I thought I married somebody that I loved unconditionally and I believed he loved me unconditionally back. That was not the case.

After working on my limiting beliefs, I understand that I only saw what I wanted to see. It was like I had a job posting that contained everything I needed from a husband. That list came from whatever I believed I needed to feel aligned and was not taking responsibility for it myself. I was looking outside of myself for a man to meet a list of needs that I believed I couldn't fulfill on my own. I was not consciously aware of any of it.

I was looking for someone who could make money because then, he could take care of me and that would make me feel safe. I was looking for someone that was physically strong because that made me feel secure. I was looking for somebody who was educated because I had the belief that if they were educated, they could get a better job and make more money and therefore take care of me. I was looking for someone with a sense of humor because when I laughed it felt good. It went on and on.

When I was with him, I was only seeing a version of him through the filters of my mind. I was filtering my experiences with him, looking for evidence that he could fulfill my needs created by my limiting beliefs. "I need to be taken care of. I need to be safe. I need to be loved."

When we got married, he met my projected needs. When he stopped meeting my needs, I'd look at him and see him as not measuring up. I'd see him as not doing what he agreed to do. However, he really didn't agree to anything. He just showed up as himself believing that I was seeing him, just as he was.

Let's move forward fourteen years. My husband says to me, "I can't handle you being disabled and I don't want to be married to you anymore. I'm in love with someone else."

Your first reaction might be, "Wow, what a horrible person!"

Let's take a closer look at what he said. "I can't handle you being disabled." He's sharing his truth. He's showing up in the moment and he's telling me what he can't handle by saying, "I can't handle being with someone who is disabled."

If I was aligned, and I loved him unconditionally, I would want him to have what he wants because, alternatively, I'd be saying, "I don't care what you want. You need to show up and love me no matter what, regardless of what you want."

It does not feel loving to tell someone else what they need to do so that I can be happy. It does not feel loving to tell someone that their feelings don't matter. That's not unconditional love.

I told everybody who'd listen, "What an asshole. What a terrible person." Unconsciously, unknowingly, I believed I needed to manipulate him, guilt him into staying with me because my happiness was at risk. I needed to be taken care of. I needed to be safe. I needed to be loved damn it, and he is the one responsible for that. He needed to stay with me and love me. "You married me. You promised to stay married for life, in sickness, and in health. So, suck it up buttercup. You need to step up and love me until you die. What you want does not matter. You need to do what I want, so I'm happy."

Isn't that crazy?

If I loved unconditionally, without my limiting beliefs interfering, I'd be able to open myself up and just hear this man speak his truth. I would have heard the pain of how he wanted to love me, disabled and all, but he couldn't. I would have understood that he loved who he loved and, in that moment, it was not me. That, who he loved was not in my control, and to manipulate or guilt him into staying, or to ask him to pretend he loved me when he didn't, would be cruel.

Let's look at the second part of what he said. I don't want to be married to you anymore. This man was speaking his truth.

He was telling me what he wanted and that was someone else. Again, my inner unconscious dialogue was, "You can't want anything other than what I want. I want you to be married to me regardless of what you want. What's important is what makes me happy and what I think makes me happy right now, is for us to stay married. I don't care that you love someone else because you told me you loved me, so you need to keep loving me. You need to keep loving me regardless if you love someone else."

Again, crazy.

If I truly loved him unconditionally, would I not want him to love who he loves? Would I not want him to be happy?

Would I not be happier to be with someone who loves me? It was actually more loving for him to have divorced me since he didn't love me than to stay married and love someone else. That was really what I was asking him to do by resisting the breakup. I was asking my reality to stay the same and be married to a man who didn't love me because somehow that would make me happy? It doesn't make sense.

When we are triggered by our LES Loops, we react and behave in ways that don't make sense.

We are in these relationships where we believe that we are loving someone unconditionally, but are we really? Or, are we loving the version of who we believe them to be? Is it not conditional love if we require people to act a certain way so we're happy?

By transforming our LES Loops, we move more into alignment where we no longer require anything from the outside because we are filled up from the inside. We are able to see the true essence of those we love, clearly, without expectations. That is unconditional love and that is who we are before we go looking for love outside of ourselves.

Chapter 8

USING THE ALIGNMENT STRATEGY

Alignment requires Awareness. Alignment is Awareness. Awareness is who you are.

I am Awareness, and as Awareness, I can observe my experience, and I can become aware of my body, how it feels, and how it is reacting. I can be aware of my emotions, and I can observe or be aware of my thoughts.

When I, as Awareness, feel, think, perceive, react, and respond from this state, mentally, emotionally, and physically it feels like peace, calm, and joy. I'm just enjoying the show. I'm in the Alignment Zone.

When I, as Awareness, feel, think, perceive, react, and respond from the mind's limited beliefs or perceptions, mentally, emotionally, and physically, it feels like discomfort, agitation, anger, sadness, or stress. I'm in the show. I'm in the Outside Zone.

I found it easier to understand how to stay in the Alignment Zone by recognizing when I was not in it. In other words,

I used discomfort as a benchmark. The more tuned in to my experience, thoughts, emotions, and physical body, the more sensitive I became to discomfort, and I used that Awareness of discomfort to initiate steps to go back inward.

How to Bring Yourself Back into The Alignment Zone

1. **When you recognize that you are feeling discomfort or negativity, acknowledge it.**

   Draw your Awareness to the sensations in your body and the emotions that are rising.

   Consider asking yourself,

   Emotionally,

   - Am I annoyed, irritated? Disgusted? Bossy? Pushy?
   - Am I angry? Mad? Swearing? Aggressive? Bitter?
   - Am I sad, displeased, hurt, depleted, exhausted, unmotivated, disconnected?
   - Am I disappointed?
   - Do I feel anxious?
   - Am I scared? Nervous? Insecure? Nervous? Guarded?
   - Am I hurt? Aching? Victimized?
   - Am I embarrassed?
   - Do I feel rejected? Overlooked?
   - Am I feeling powerless? Overwhelmed? Incapable? Weak? Paralyzed?
   - Am I feeling small?
   - Am I feeling depressed? Self-critical? Lousy? Burdened?
   - Am I feeling distrustful? Unsure? Shy? Hesitant?
   - Am I feeling numb? Cold? Uncaring?

- Am I lonely? Unhappy?

Physically,

- Is my body tense?
- Has my breathing changed? Quickened?
- Am I holding my breath?
- Are my hands clenched?
- Is my jaw tight?
- Does my neck hurt?
- Do I have an upset stomach?
- Does my heart feel empty?
- Are my muscles tense?
- Do I have a furrowed brow?
- Am I getting hot?
- Are my teeth clenched?
- Do I feel sweaty?
- Do I want to vomit?
- Am I trembling?
- Am I stiff?

For example, imagine yourself waiting for your friend George to join you for lunch, and he is late. Being aware of your experience might sound something like this, "I feel angry, annoyed, my cheeks feel hot, my neck is tense, my brow is furrowed. I am angry at George for being late. I feel disrespected, not important, overlooked."

Record your observations on your phone or in a journal.

2. **Isolate the thought or thoughts you believe to be true.**

You see, there is always a thought that precipitates a negative emotion. The thought is what is triggering the emotion.

Consider asking yourself,

- ◦ What am I believing to be true?
- ◦ Am I judging the situation or a person?
- ◦ Do I want someone to change so I can be happy? What do they need to change?
- ◦ Do I want someone to do something different so I won't be upset? What are they doing that is upsetting? If they are doing that, what kind of person does that make them?
- ◦ Am I comparing myself to others?
- ◦ Am I trying to be right? Pointing out what is wrong?
- ◦ Do I want to tell other people what happened? Gossip?
- ◦ Am I trying to make myself appear better than someone else?
- ◦ Am I trying to make myself appear smaller than someone else?
- ◦ Am I trying to control the conversation?
- ◦ Am I focused on what should not be happening?

Some of the thoughts might be, George is late. George disrespected me. George annoys me. George makes me angry. George makes me mad. George is annoying. George needs to be on time. George needs to respect me.

Record your observations on your phone or in a journal.

3. Isolate the strategies you are using to deal with the emotions.

What behaviors or actions do you take when you feel negative emotions.

Consider asking yourself,

- Have I had this type of experience before?
- Have I responded like this in the past?
    - ◦ If so, what proceeded the response?

    - What would I be afraid of happening if I no longer responded that way?
- What do I hope to achieve by acting this way?
- What experience am I trying to prevent from happening?
    - What impact would that experience have?
    - How would it affect me?

When George was late, I got quiet. I didn't share what I was thinking. I held back. I was disengaged from the conversation. I made noises with the menu. I gave him the silent treatment. I didn't share with him that I was angry. I told him not to worry about being late. I made sure he was happy.

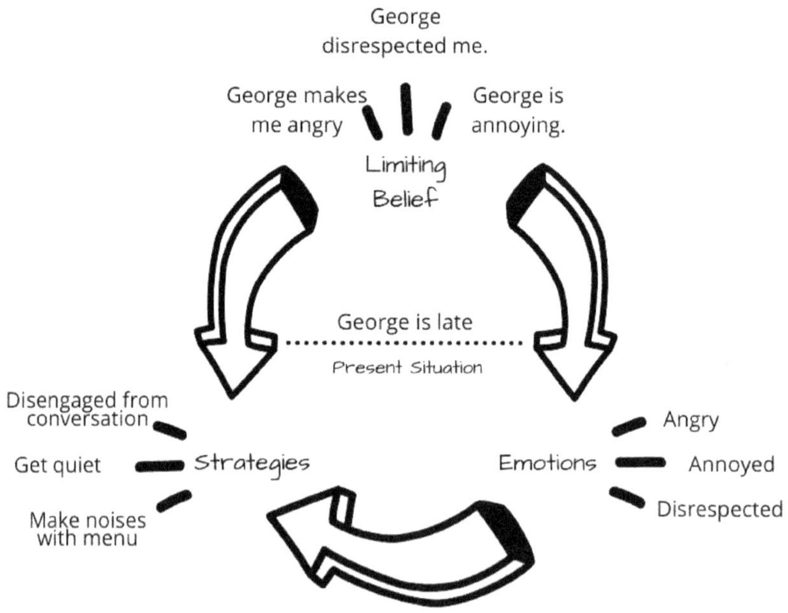

4. Find new, more positive thoughts that embrace an alternate perception.

Take a thought and find alternate perceptions that could be just as true. If the thought was George is annoying, some alternate perceptions could be George doesn't annoy me, George helps me, George is a great friend, George is a blessing.

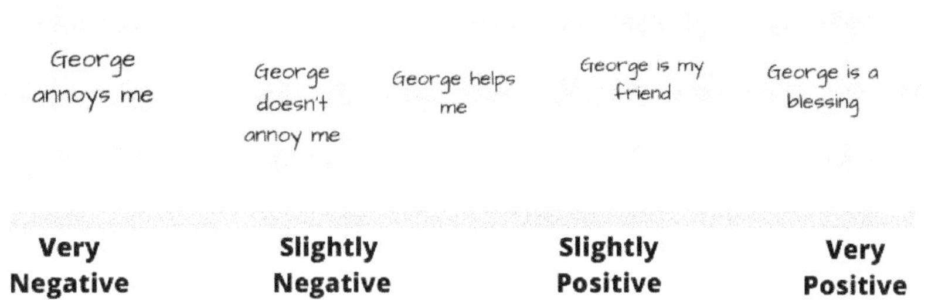

The idea is to keep doing this until you move back into the Alignment Zone. If you can, record your observations on your phone or in a journal.

At first, this may seem difficult because your brain is super focused on one way of looking at things, and in this case, it would be that George was late and was responsible for you being annoyed.

5. Find examples to support an alternate, more positive thought.

Once you have entertained alternate, more positive perceptions, it is crucial to find real examples of how those new perceptions could be just as true or truer. Finding proof helps to anchor the new perception in your brain and gives it emotional power to counter-balance the negative thought and the negatively charged evidence attached to the negative thoughts. I find that my anger and annoyance dissolves as

I gradually move back into the Alignment Zone with each thought of positivity.

Example:

Limiting Belief - George is annoying.

Alternate perception - George is not annoying.
Evidence

- He is not there because he was late so he can't be annoying.
- I laugh in his company, and I love that.
- I have lunch with him because I like talking with him.

Alternate perception - George doesn't annoy me.
Evidence

- George was not there, so he couldn't be the one annoying me.
- My thoughts were telling a story and triggered annoyance emotions within me. Not George.
- He has been there for me many times when I needed a friend

Alternate perception - George helps me.
Evidence

- When he doesn't react to my quietness, I can better observe my behavior.
- When he is late, I can notice how I am triggering my LES Loops
- When he moved my furniture last month.

Alternate perception - George is my friend.
Evidence

- He came to have lunch with me
- Perhaps he was late because he was busy but still found the time to come to lunch.
- He puts up with my menu banging behavior.

Alternate perception - George is a blessing.
Evidence

- He came to have lunch with me
- He stayed to have lunch with me even though I was disengaged.
- He puts up with my menu banging, not saying anything about my behavior.

6. **Recite a running dialogue of positive self-talk.**
   Get your brain to consider,

   - What am I gaining?
   - How is this for me?
   - What gifts am I receiving?

Use your answers to those questions, and all of the alternate positive perceptions and evidential support you found in #5 above, to create a running dialogue. It might sound something like this.

"I can take this time and check in to see what my body

would like for lunch. I can spend time taking in the decor and feel the sun coming through the window and warm my skin. I can trust that George is doing what George needs to be doing in this moment, just as I am doing what I need to be doing in this moment. I connect with my breathing. I can smell the aroma of the food being brought out of the kitchen. How exciting that I have the money to go out for lunch. How fascinating that I thought I was having lunch with someone, and I am now eating alone. I wonder how eating alone is perfect for me in this moment. What am I gaining? How is this for me? How am I growing, expanding?"

I would keep doing that until I moved into the Alignment Zone. That way, when George arrived, I'd be in my natural state of peace and calm, clearly seeing the magnificence of who he really was, and I'd know that he arrived exactly when he was supposed to have come. I'd have considered all the gifts that I received because of his delayed arrival, including the opportunity to transform an old limiting belief.

7. Can I find the first Loop?

I projected my discomfort onto George by making him responsible for it. I'm experiencing discomfort because he was late. I can now take that projection and use the mirroring technique. From the first Loop, I chose the limiting Belief, "George is annoying," and converted it to the mirrored Belief, "I am annoying," for the center of the next Mirrored Belief Loop. I could have used the "I" statement, "I am late," for George is late. "I make George angry," or "I make myself angry," for George is angry. Or, I could have used the mirrored beliefs, "I disrespected George," or "I disrespected myself," for George disrespected me. "I annoy myself" is another possible "I" statement for, George annoys me.

I would suggest picking out the Belief that either jumps out at you or feels the heaviest. The mirrored Belief that needs to be worked on usually stands out somehow, but when in doubt, do all of them individually using the mirrored LES Loop template.

Remember, it's the attachment to a thought within me that creates the discomfort I am experiencing, not George. Once I attach to a thought, it starts making connections to other negative thoughts, which triggers negative emotions and old patterned responses, triggering a LES Loop.

> **Present Day Experience:** George is late.
> **Liming Belief**: George disrespected me. George is annoying. George makes me angry.
> **Mirrored Beliefs**: I am late. I disrespect George. I am disrespectful. I disrespect me. I am annoying. I annoy George. I am angry. I make George angry.
> **Emotions**: Annoyed, ignored, overlooked, disrespected
> **Strategy**: Disengage, get quiet, make noises like huffing and puffing with my breath, slamming things.

Using Mirroring To Find A LES Loop

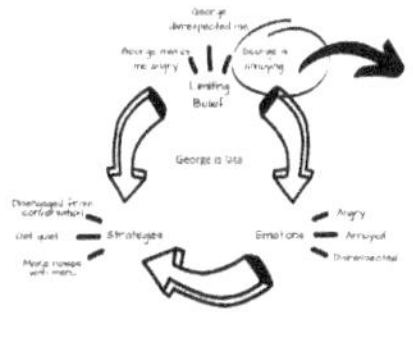

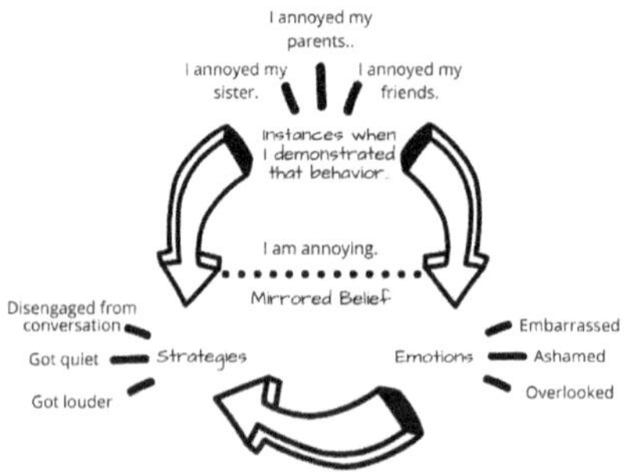

If I criticize George as being annoying, George is mirroring back to me that I need to work on the Belief, "I am annoying." It means that there is a LES Loop active within me, and I am using criticism as a strategy to resist having to feel the emotions associated with the times in my life when I was annoying. When someone's behavior reminds me of times when I was annoying, it triggers the old emotions from my past within me. If I can open myself up to the experiences where I believed I was annoying, I can move back into Alignment. I can ask myself, were there times in my life when I thought I was annoying? Yes. Absolutely. How did it make me feel? What strategies did I use back then to deal with those emotions?

Memory of a time I was annoying - I was annoying when I used to sing for my parents, and I remember them laughing behind their newspaper. I was annoying them.

Emotions - Ignored, overlooked, frustrated, unloved

Did that strategy play out here during lunch? Yes. By being late, I felt overlooked, not important.

Strategy - I sang louder

Did that strategy play out here during lunch? - Yes. I banged the menu, loudly.

Memory of a time I was annoying. I annoyed my sister so she moved out of our shared bedroom.

Emotions - Rejected, unloved, discarded

Did that strategy play out here during lunch? Yes. I felt I was not important enough for George to be on time.

Strategy - Got quiet.

Did that strategy play out here during lunch? Yes. I got quiet.

Memory of a time I was annoying. I was annoying when I first got diagnosed with Muscular Dystrophy and talked about my problems.

Emotions - Embarrassed, ashamed, not important.

Did those emotions arise at lunch? Yes. I felt embarrassed to be sitting alone at lunch and not important enough for George to be on time. Something else took precedence over me.

Strategy - Stopped sharing

Did that strategy play out here during lunch? Yes. I disengaged from the conversation.

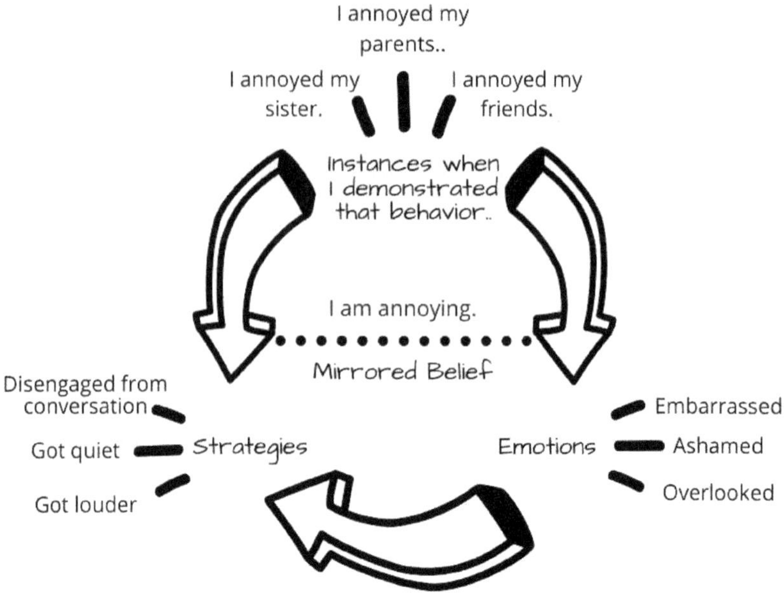

Feeling ignored, rejected, or overlooked was common in the past scenarios above, and those same emotions were being triggered by George being late. My mind created a perception of what it meant that George was late.

My mind thought, I am alone. George is supposed to join me for lunch. George is not here. George is late. George disrespected me. George makes me angry. George makes me mad. George annoys me.

When George was late, I believed I was being ignored, which triggered old loops, emotions, and strategies, including the projection that George caused my discomfort. Sitting at the restaurant, I attached to the limiting Belief, "George is late," and that attachment moved me out of the Alignment Zone.

Being annoyed had nothing to do with George and everything to do with my interpretation of sitting alone in the restaurant and making connections to old LES Loops. Ultimately, my experience of George's arrival time was utterly dependent on whether or not I was in the Alignment Zone.

8. Question the limiting beliefs from the earliest instance.

By questioning the limiting Belief associated with the earliest instance of me believing that I was annoying, I can reduce or eliminate the LES Loop's power to influence my present-day experience.

Limiting Belief: I annoyed my sister.

When I sit with the thought, "I annoy my sister," while in Alignment and while believing that I am the divine plan unfolding, the answer gently rises within me, "no."

Is that true? No

Alternate Perceptions: I did not annoy my sister. I do not annoy my sister.

What examples or memories rose up that contradicted my limiting belief?

1. She was older and wanted her privacy.
2. She might have wanted to have friends over so they could hang out in her room privately.
3. She was going through puberty, and that made her uncomfortable.

I am considering that there were alternate reasons for her feeling annoyed that had nothing to do with me.

Again, by exploring the infinite perceptions available to me, I can bring myself further into the Alignment Zone and begin to soften. I can begin to see that I am not annoying and that there were thousands of perceptual possibilities of why my sister wanted her own room. One of them could have been that I was annoying her. If that was the case, she had a triggered LES Loop within her, which was her responsibility. She was out of Alignment, and her annoyance had nothing to do with me.

9. Rewrite my story

I can rewrite the story with a new understanding of how the earliest experience could have been perceived differently.

From the vantage point of an adult, I see that I am not annoying. The belief that I am annoying came from a child's desire to be around her big sister because it made her feel loved, and she did not realize that her sister could love her without wanting to share a room with her. That young child didn't realize that her natural state was love, and she didn't need her sister to elicit that feeling within her. As an adult, I enjoy my privacy and having my own room, and it has nothing to do with other people. I am just like my sister.

Alignment Strategy – Spilled Coffee

Let's say I'm grabbing my coffee at the drive-through on my way to work and it spills down the front of my shirt. I immediately look down and swear loudly.

If we refer to the diagram, I went from ordering coffee in the Alignment Zone to resistance in the Outside Zone.

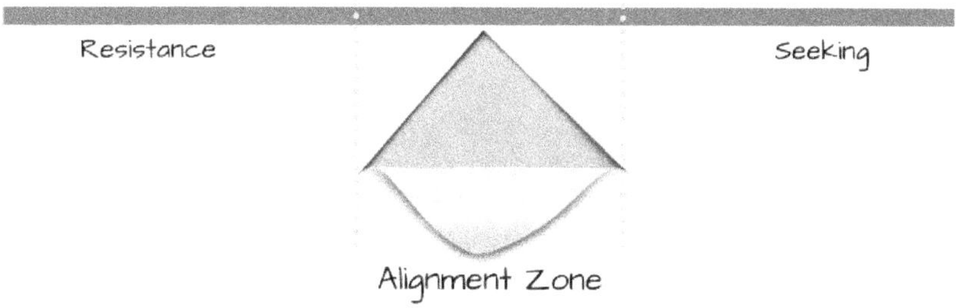

1. When I recognize that I am feeling discomfort or negativity, acknowledge it.

When the coffee spilled my body tensed up, and I felt angry and annoyed.

2. Isolate the thought or thoughts I believe to be true.

My brain connected, spilling coffee on my shirt as a bad situation. My brain processed a split-second summary of a plethora of thoughts like, "My shirt. It's ruined. I can't go to work like this. Now I'll be late. My boss will be mad. I'll get fired. I can't go home. I don't have time. I can't believe this happened. Everything always happens to me. I can't afford another shirt."

3. **Isolate the strategies you are using to deal with the emotions.**

I swore. I blamed the employee who served the coffee. After cleaning up the spill and dousing my shirt with water, I may move back to the Alignment Zone naturally, but if the negative feeling doesn't shift, I can use the Alignment Strategy to bring me back to my natural state.

4. **Find new, more positive thoughts that embrace an alternate perception.**

For example, a more positive alternate thought than "My shirt is ruined" might be, "My shirt is not ruined." This is slightly less negative than the original negative thought and can draw me back towards the Alignment Zone. The closer I get to the Alignment Zone, the easier it will be to affirm more positive perceptions such as, "My shirt did a great job absorbing the spill. My shirt protected my skin. The Universe was letting me know I needed a new shirt."

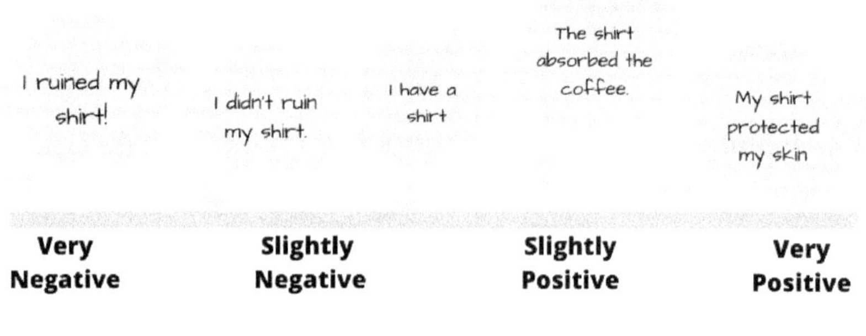

This process often doesn't work for people because they believe they need to feel over the top ecstatic about spilling their coffee on themselves for this process to work. That's not the case. We are looking to bring ourselves back to our natural state of peace and calm. I can ask myself, how is this for me? What gifts am I receiving? What might be gained? How am I supported, loved, growing, expanding, evolving in this moment because life happens for me, there is always a gift, I am safe, whole loved, and supported, always.

We always have the ability to choose an alternate way of perceiving our experience.

5. Find examples to support an alternate, more positive thought.

Once I have entertained alternate, more positive perceptions, I find real examples of how these new perceptions could be just as true or truer. This process helps to anchor the new perception in my brain and gives it emotional power to help counter-balance the negative thought and the negatively charged evidence attached to it.

Something like this:

Example:

Limiting Belief – My shirt is ruined

Alternate perception - My shirt is not ruined

Evidence

- I've had clothes that have had stains before, and the stains came out.
- The rest of the shirt is fine.
- I can wear it again when I paint. Therefore, it is still usable.

Limiting Belief – I can't go to work like this.

Alternate perception - I can go to work like this.

Evidence

- I've spilled on my shirt at work before.
- What my shirt looks like has nothing to do with me being able to go to work.
- The stain on my shirt does not prevent me from driving.

Limiting Belief – Everything always happens to me.

Alternate perception - Everything doesn't always happen to me.

Evidence

- I've gotten a coffee before, and it didn't spill on me.
- Some things happen to other people and not me.
- Only whatever is supposed to happen to me happens to me.

6. Recite a running dialogue of positive self-talk.

Next, I use all the positive thoughts, affirmations, and evidential support to create a running dialogue. It might sound something like this,

> *My shirt is not ruined. It's just wet and needs spot cleaner. I needed a new shirt anyway. This is the Universe telling me it is time to get a new shirt. I can go to work like this. What my shirt looks like has nothing to do with me being able to go to work. I'll have a great story to tell at the water cooler. Hey everybody, has this ever happened to you? I won't be late if I go to work in this shirt. I can choose to go to work with a coffee stain and be on time. I'm always where I need to be at the perfect time. The Universe ensures I am exactly where I need to be. Everything doesn't happen to me. Some things happen to other people and not me, like being elected President. I'm in the flow with whatever happens, like a raft floating in the lake. I*

can afford another shirt, especially if I stop buying coffee. I am grateful to have a shirt. How great is it that I have other shirts to wear if the one I'm wearing gets wet!

In my experience, after I repeat the affirmations in the running dialogue, I'm back into Alignment and feel good again. Or at least, better than I felt before. You see, every thought has an emotion attached to it. If I have negative thoughts, I am going to feel negative. There is nothing wrong with feeling negative, but I don't enjoy myself when I feel negative. That's why I love using this technique to bring myself back into Alignment. I get to choose how I feel regardless of what is happening outside of me.

I know you're probably thinking, "I don't have time to find all those affirmations." I get that. One thing you can do is have a "Go-To," affirmation dialogue, or mantra prepared and ready ahead of time that you can use no matter what the situation. You can just repeat those affirmations until you feel your energy shift. To create your own, "Go-To" affirmations, consider statements that are positive. For example, some general affirmations that could be applied to any situation might be:

- I choose to move through this with ease.
- Solutions always exist, and I am open to receive them.
- This moment is integral to a bigger plan.
- I am always growing and expanding.
- This experience is for my growth and expansion.
- I have all the answers within me.
- Any negative reaction is drawing me inward to identify the limiting beliefs keeping me from tapping into my natural state of peace and calm.
- There is always a gift in every experience.

The thing is, I can give you some general affirmations, but what works is a list of affirmations that are created by you because they will be familiar, a part of your personal prose, and they'll slide off your tongue a bit easier.

Be careful that the positive affirmations you come up with are not actually negative. For instance, the affirmation, "I choose to move through this with less stress," is not a positively charged affirmation. The word stress is just that, stressful, and it carries with it a negative charge. Instead, use a positive word. If you were less stressed, what would you be experiencing instead? Maybe peace or a sense of calm? The affirmation would be more positively charged using those words and more effective at shifting you into the Alignment Zone. The affirmation might be, "I will move through this peacefully and calmly, I calmly move through this experience or, I choose to be calm and peaceful."

7. Can I find the first Loop?

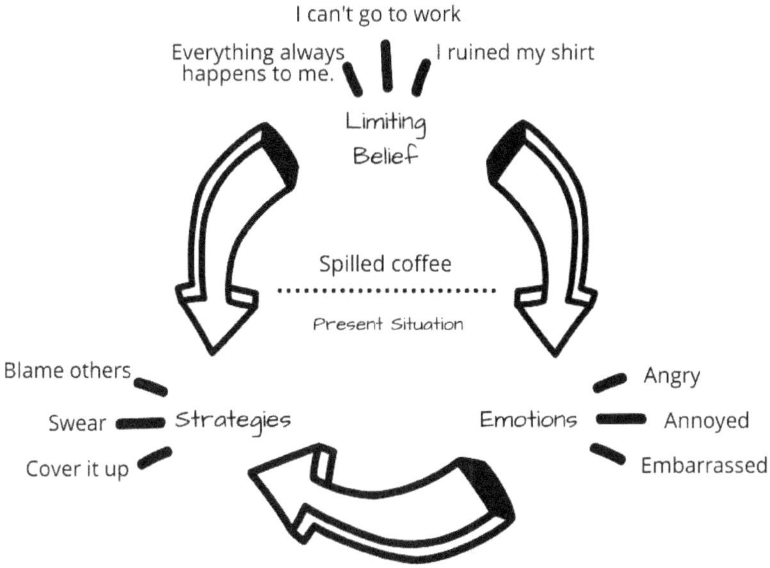

I projected onto my shirt that it was ruined, and that projection created discomfort. I can now take that projection, and using the mirroring technique, place the thought in the center of the LES Loop. The limiting beliefs can be mirrored to create "I" Statements.

> "Everything always happens to me," mirrored, is, "Everything always happens to me."
> "I can't go to work," mirrored, is, "I can't go," or "I can't go to work."
> "I ruined my shirt," mirrored, is, "I am ruined."

I chose "I am ruined" to take to the next Loop, but I could have used "I can't work, I don't work, and everything always happens to me" as well. I would suggest picking out the belief that either jumps out at you or feels the heaviest. The mirrored belief that needs to be worked on usually stands out somehow, but when in doubt, do all of them individually using the mirrored Loop.

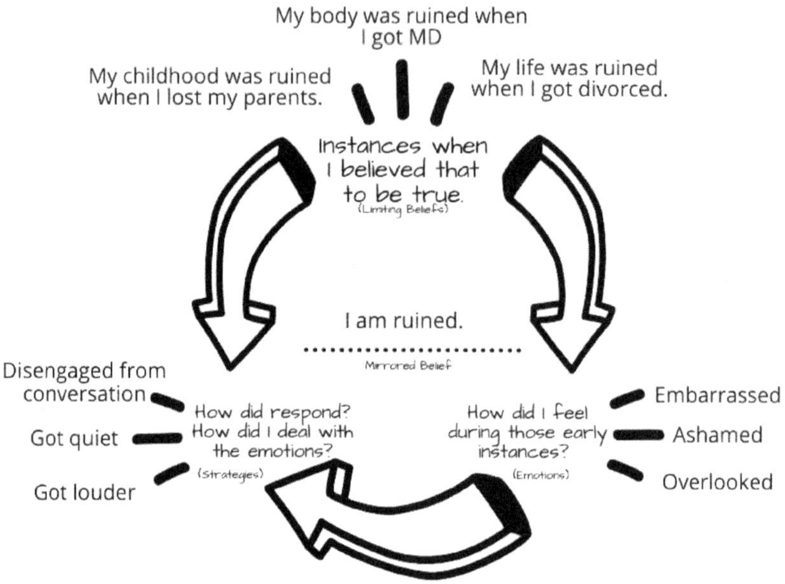

Sometimes by doing the LES Loops, other memories or connections get made, and it is important to record them. When I was going through this random example of spilling coffee for this book, I made significant personal connections in the mirrored belief loop and also with the earliest memory loop below.

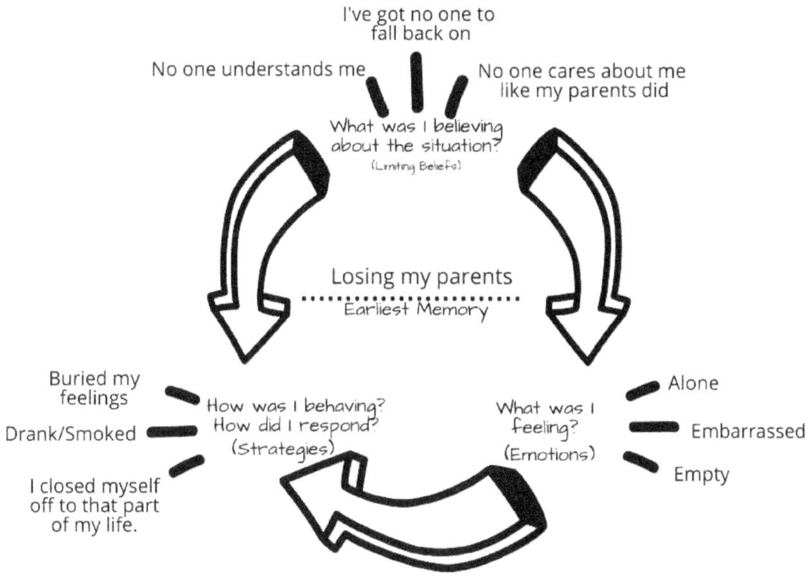

8. Question the limiting beliefs from the earliest instance.

By questioning the limiting Belief associated with the earliest instance of me believing that I've got no one to fall back on, I can reduce or eliminate the power of the LES Loop to influence my present-day experience.

Limiting Belief: I've got no one to fall back on.

When I sit with the thought, "I've got no one to fall back on," while in Alignment and believing that I am the divine plan unfolding, the answer gently rises within me, "no."

Is that true? No. Where did that answer come from? What memories rose up within me? What other possible perceptions came to light?

Alternate possible perceptions of the earliest memory: I have people to fall back on. I did have people to fall back on.

What examples or memories rose up that contradicted my limiting belief?

1. I had my friend's parents that I could fall back on.
2. I had my brothers and sister to fall back on.
3. I had me to fall back on

Limiting Belief: No one cares about me as my parents did.

Is it true? No

Alternate possible perceptions of the earliest memory: People care about me as my parents did. People did care about me as my parents did.

What examples or memories rose up that contradicted my limiting belief?

1. I can't know the level that my parents cared about me because that was in their minds.
2. Whether or not "I feel cared about" is in my head and determined by my limiting beliefs. Therefore, I can't know for sure how much I am cared for.
3. I know how much I cared about my parents, and therefore, my children might care for me as much as my parents did.

Limiting Belief: No one understands me.

Is it true? No

Alternate possible perceptions of the earliest memory: People do understand me. People did understand me.

What examples or memories rose up that contradicted my limiting belief?

1. My parents could understand what I was saying. They understood English.
2. They understood what I wanted but didn't think I needed protection. They knew I was safe even if I didn't.
3. My brother understood that his teasing me got a reaction. He understood my triggers. He understood me.

9. Rewrite the Story.

I can rewrite the story with a new understanding of how the earliest experience could have been perceived differently.

I have always had someone to fall back on, and that person is me. I can fall back on me to choose Alignment over all else and can do this work to understand my thinking, my emotions, and my behavior. I have had me to fall back on my whole life. I am surrounded by people who love and care about me, and if I do need them, I could fall back on them. I am always supported, always taken care of, and trust that if I need to fall back on something or someone, they'll be there because I always have exactly what I need.

You might be thinking, "Really? This early memory loop is responsible for swearing over a spilled coffee? Can't I just swear because I spilled my coffee?"

Some people can spill a coffee and just clean it up. No reaction, just the gentle inner calling to clean up the spill. They remain in Alignment and do not attach to any limiting beliefs. Other people swear and react automatically based on triggered loops. One reaction maintains your Alignment with your natural state of peace and calm, and one reaction draws you out of Alignment with your natural state.

Alignment Strategy – I'm Angry

In the year 2000, I believed that I was a shining example of someone who was generally cool, calm, and collected because I rarely showed negative emotion. That's why I was surprised when Brenda, an intuitive I was seeing, told me that I was angry. I thought, "If you're looking for anger, then you should talk to my husband. He's the one with all the anger issues." However, it was my denial of anger that conveyed to me that I was indeed angry.

1. When I recognize that I am feeling discomfort or negativity, acknowledge it.

I thought, "Where's the anger? Am I angry at Mom? Am I angry at Dad? Am I angry at my husband? Am I angry at God?" I didn't feel angry or tense. Nothing came to me.
The intuitive suggested that one day when I was alone at home, to take a bat and hit my bed with it, allowing whatever came up to come up and to say whatever I wanted to say out loud. So, I grabbed my bat, swung it up above my head, and smashed it down onto the mattress, intending to find the anger. I yelled out whatever came to mind with each hit. At first, it felt awkward, foreign, and uncomfortable, but I kept at it until finally, something came out.

2. Isolate the thought or thoughts I believe to be true.

"I hate being sick. I hate not being able to do what I want. I hate that my Mom and Dad died. I hate that I feel alone. I hate that I hurt. I hate that my husband had an affair. I hate feeling sad all the time." I started hitting harder and yelling louder. "I hate being in a state of chaos. I hate God. I hate that it doesn't matter what I do because something bad always happens to me." I had allowed the container deep inside to open up and free the buried anger from years ago. Tears formed, and my insides loosened as I released more and more with each hit. "I hate that no one really loves me." My body began to feel lighter, and the sensation of sleepiness came over me. All the energy used to hold in and deny the anger seemed to be released and suddenly available.

By freely feeling and expressing the anger within me, I had allowed that buried emotion to surface and be released. I no longer needed to hold it in, conceal or suppress it because I was inviting it to be part of me rather than resisting and denying that it existed.

Later, in a calmer state, I could take each statement that I expressed aloud and isolate the limiting beliefs.

Limiting Beliefs:

I am sick.
I can't share my emotions.
I shouldn't have muscular dystrophy.
I can't do what I want.
I should be doing something different than what I am doing.
My parents should not have died.
I am alone.
I hurt.
My husband should not have had an affair.
I am sad all the time.
I am in a state of chaos.
God is mean.
It doesn't matter what I do.
Bad things always happen to me.
No one really loves me.

3. Isolate the strategies I am using to deal with the emotions

I pushed my feelings down inside and buried them. I ignored them.

4. Find new, more positive thoughts that embrace an alternate perception.

Next, I could try to find positive, alternative perceptions for the limiting beliefs.

For example, positive, alternative thoughts for, "I am sick," could be...

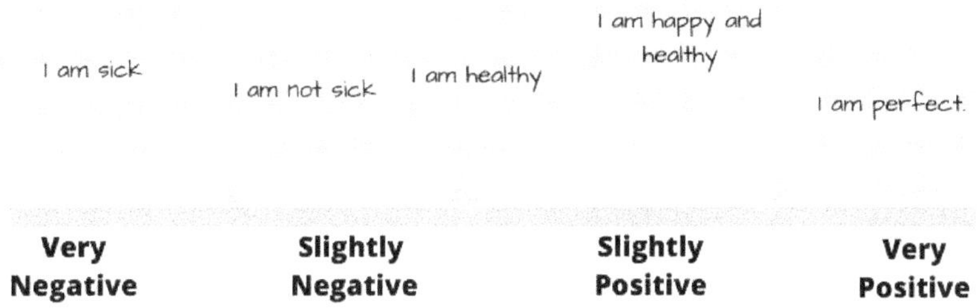

Other possible perceptions:

I am free.
I can do what I want.
I am being done.
I should be doing what I am doing.
My parents should have died.
My parents are still with me.
I am not alone.
I am surrounded by friends and family.
I don't hurt.

I feel great.
My husband should have had an affair.
My divorce opened me up to who I really am.
My husband having an affair was a blessing.
I am not sad all the time.
I am happy.
My life is organized.
God is love.
It does matter what I do.
Bad things do not always happen to me.
Good things always happen to me.
Good things happen to me.
I am loved.

5. Find examples to support an alternate, more positive thought.

Next, I would take each new positive perception and find proof to help anchor it in possibility. That would help to move me from the Outside Zone towards the Alignment Zone.

For example,

Limiting Belief - I am sick.
New positive perception - I am not sick.
Evidence

- I can work.
- I am not taking any medications.
- I can take care of things at home and work.

Limiting Belief - I can't share my emotions.

New positive perception - I allow my emotions to flow in and out of my experience freely.

Evidence

- I banged on the pillow and let them out.
- I laugh freely.
- I cry during sad movies.

6. Recite a running dialogue of positive self-talk.

> *I am healthy and whole just as I am. My emotions support my growth and expansion to understand my limiting beliefs and LES Loops. I am grateful for my emotions because they allow me to feel love, kindness, compassion, and passion. My feelings help me detect Limiting Beliefs and help me recognize when I am out of Alignment. I choose to allow my emotions to rise up and out of me. The strategy I was using to suppress my emotions no longer serves me.*

7. Can I find the first Loop?

When I look at the first LES Loop below, what jumps out at me is the Limiting Belief that my parents should not have died. It is possible that was the first time I suppressed my anger and created the initial LES Loop. As a child, I did not feel that I could share my anger for fear of upsetting my mother, so I kept my feelings to myself.

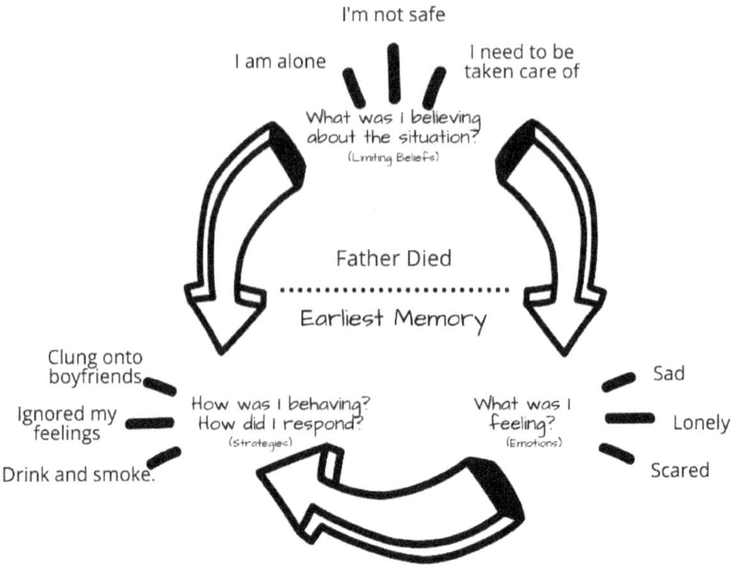

After making the connection between anger, feeling sad, lonely, and scared as a child, I can bring Awareness to my reactions and be on the lookout for old strategies. If I notice I am ignoring my feelings, I can choose to express them. If I notice I want to cling or want to find a new relationship, I can choose to align myself first, then decide. If I notice I am criticizing others for being angry, I can complete the LES templates.

8. Question the limiting beliefs from the earliest instance.

I now take each belief from the Earliest Memory Loop and ask myself, "Is it true?" I need to sit with it while in Alignment, knowing I am the divine plan unfolding. This was probably where the LES Loop originated, and it was created from the mindset of a child.

Limiting Belief: I'm not safe.

Looking back on that situation, was I not safe? What is my definition of safe? Safe from death? Safe from starvation? Safe from injury? Safe from lions? Was I left in the wild? I can find instances when I was indeed safe from death, starvation, injury, and lions, so, no, it is not true that I was not safe.

Is that true? No

Alternate possible perceptions of the earliest memory: I am safe. I was safe.

What examples or memories rose up that contradicted my limiting belief?

1. I'm alive now, over 30 years later, so I must have been safe.
2. I had food, water, and shelter that kept me safe.
3. I was not being harmed, so I was safe.

Limiting Belief: I am alone.

Looking back on that situation, was I alone? Was I left entirely alone? Was there no one around? Ever? Was I the only one on the planet? I can find instances when there were people around me; therefore, no, it is not true that I was alone.

Is that true? No

Alternate possible perceptions of the earliest memory: I am not alone. I was not alone.

What examples or memories rose up that contradicted my limiting belief?

1. I had my mother. I was not alone.

2. I had friends and my friend's parents. I was not alone.

3. I chose to live on my own, even though people offered to have me stay with them.

Limiting Belief: I need to be taken care of.

Looking back on that situation, did I need to be taken care of? Did I need someone to feed me? Cloth me? Speak for me? Make decisions for me? I can find instances when I took care of myself confidently and without assistance.

Is that true? No

Alternate possible perceptions of the earliest memory: I don't need to be taken care of. I was taken care of.

What examples or memories rose up that contradicted my limiting belief?

1. I live on my own, so I don't need to be taken care of.

2. I represented myself in court, so I didn't need to be taken care of.

3. It is 30 years later, and I'm fine, so that means I didn't need anyone to take care of me.

9. Rewrite the story.

I was safe, had people to support me, and was taken care of always, regardless if my father was there or not there. As a little girl, I believed it was my father that made me safe, loved, and cared for, but I was that already.

As an adult, I can see more and open myself up to how I am safe in each moment. This is my truth. This is what I choose to believe now. As an adult, I can recognize an infinite number of perceptions of what could be true rather than the narrow, limited version I perceived as a child.

As an adult, I choose to be aligned and consider what loving action I'm being called to take. I no longer choose to react habitually, automatically, and from an unaligned state.

The Alignment Strategy - Coronavirus

Writing this amid a pandemic is a great time to highlight how the Alignment Strategy can help keep people aligned, clear, and open through a challenge rather than being reactive and stressed.

The Coronavirus outbreak is an example of how outside circumstances can trigger emotional reactions and behavioral responses linked to our past. When I look around, watch the news, or read about the accounts of individuals maneuvering their way through the uncharted territory of a pandemic, it is fascinating to me how some people are going about their day as though nothing has changed and others are petrified of running out of toilet paper.

Discomfort and stress are the first indications signaling the presence of active limiting beliefs. Some people have difficulty imagining that it is possible to be in the middle of a pandemic and not be stressed out about it.

However, it is possible to experience the Coronavirus outbreak from a state of peace and calm by staying in The Alignment Zone. By perceiving the outside world from an aligned space, individuals can take in information from the outside and act consciously and clearly from a place of love and compassion.

For instance, if I maintain Alignment with my true self without attaching to any particular thought, I can separate or filter the information clearly, objectively, and with understanding. If the health experts advise everyone not to travel unless absolutely necessary, then that seems like a reasonable, clear choice for me as it relates to me traveling. I won't do it. That feels loving. It seems loving not to expose myself to the virus unnecessarily, and it feels loving to reduce the possibility of spreading the infection to those at high risk of experiencing complications. If the health experts suggest that it is now safe to travel, then since they are the experts, that seems like a reasonable, clear choice for me as it relates to me traveling and I may travel. Using the Alignment Strategy, I can bring Awareness to the facts and determine my behavior as it relates to the present moment, clearly from the loving essence of who I really am. I was going on a trip, and then I wasn't going on a trip.

If I experience discomfort, stress, anxiety, fear, worry, etc., that lets me know a limiting belief or beliefs have been triggered, and I am responding based on my past. For example, I was planning on going away for a school break with my children. Tickets were purchased, bags were packed, and millions of fresh, clear images of me sitting on a lounge chair sipping a margarita on a beach occupied my mind. However, let's suppose I hear the announcement that the government has recommended that no one travel outside the country. Moving forward from that moment on has less to do with the announcement and everything to do with my interpretation of it. Will I maintain Alignment in the Alignment Zone and respond clearly and calmly or will I attach to limiting beliefs and move out of the Alignment Zone? The important thing to remember is that even though I may initially struggle with the idea of a change in travel plans, I can at any moment choose to move back into the Alignment Zone if I moved out of it. Here's how I could move back into Alignment in 9 steps.

1. When you recognize that you are feeling discomfort or negativity, acknowledge it.

I would take a second and check-in. I would bring Awareness to my body and tune in to my emotions. By recognizing the disappointment and how it was showing up in my body, I could consciously determine that my reaction, sadness, shoulders slumped, face drooped, disappointment, was reflective of triggered limiting beliefs. I would know instantly that I had attached to limiting beliefs in that moment, had moved away from clarity, and was less accurately able to recognize the facts.

Therefore, identifying that I had moved out of the Alignment Zone, I could then consider not making big decisions in that moment and instead choose to wait until I had moved back in or at least closer to my natural state.

2. Isolate the thoughts or thought you believe to be true.

Next, I would bring my Awareness inward to the thoughts my brain was processing. In a triggered moment, my mind narrowly interprets the available data. By sitting quietly, paying attention, and observing any shift out of the Alignment Zone, I could then identify and follow any thoughts linking to other thoughts and record them. Some examples might be,

- The government is overreacting.
- I spent all that money.
- Will I get my money back?
- Will our insurance cover us if we still go.
- I really needed a vacation.
- Everything always happens to me.
- I didn't need this right now.
- I needed a vacation to de-stress.
- Not going on a vacation that has already been paid for is a waste of money.
- I needed a vacation for my mental health.
- Going on vacation increases family time.

By writing the thoughts down, it would allow my brain to stop processing them in thought form and allow me the opportunity to utilize other tools to transform them and help me move back into the Alignment Zone.

The greatest gift of a pandemic seems to be that it can't be ignored. It prevents my brain from living life on autopilot and instead brings any limiting beliefs or fears operating on a subconscious level up to a conscious level to be seen and dealt with.

3. Isolate the strategies you are using to deal with the emotions.

The emotion triggered by a limiting belief creates discomfort, and our brain will often implement a strategy or behavioral response to get rid of it. By bringing Awareness to how we are behaving at the signs of discomfort, we can identify old, outdated strategies that may no longer serve us.

> I'm trying to prepare for different outcomes.
> I'm eating more junk food.
> I took on a new project and am working incessantly.

In the past, I would have continually processed the stressful thoughts surrounding a pandemic, to the point where I couldn't sleep. Now, I would probably ask myself, "Have I responded like this in the past? What does it remind me of? Am I responding in a habitual strategic way?"

By bringing my Awareness inward, recording my thoughts, emotions, and the strategies that may be playing out, I can use the information to transform the old limiting beliefs and choose alternate strategies that support my Alignment. I may not be able to do that right then and there but could choose to look at them later when I had moved back into the Alignment Zone.

4. Find new, more positive thoughts that embrace an alternate perception.

Suppose my incessant thinking continued to draw me further and further away from my natural state of Alignment. In that case, I could draw myself back into the Alignment Zone by entertaining more positive thoughts or perceptions. Some alternate positive perceptions could be, "I'm glad I found out now before we were at the airport. I won't get a sunburn. I avoided being stranded in a foreign country and it could have cost me more money. Staying home is less stressful than traveling during a pandemic. Not going on vacation saves money. I get to spend an extra two weeks with my kids.
With each alternate positive thought, I can move closer to being aligned with my natural state.

5. Find examples to support an alternate, more positive thought.

I would then find specific examples of how the alternate perspectives were just as valid or if not more reasonable, than the original negative thoughts.

For example, it can be less stressful not going on vacation because I wouldn't have to deal with long line ups and screening upon my return. I wouldn't need to concern myself with whether or not airports were closed, the cost of restricted or changed flights, and increased healthcare costs abroad.

By finding examples, I can empower the alternate perceptions to stand up against the emotionally charged limiting beliefs of my past.

6. Recite a running dialogue of positive self-talk.

To maintain my movement back into The Alignment Zone, it would be beneficial to continue to think, speak, feel, and behave positively using all the tools and information discussed previously. I could do that by repeating a running dialogue of how staying home would be the best thing that could ever happen to me.

> *Staying home would be less stressful. I would not have to concern myself with being quarantined when I get back and could enjoy social distancing instead. I could relax at home. I would save the money previously earmarked for excursions. I could do those projects at home that I have been ignoring. I will avoid the potential costs of airports closing and needing to change flights or potential increased healthcare costs abroad. I will have access to amazing hospitals in my home country. I have access to family, friends, and resources in my community. I can decrease the risk of contracting the virus. I am healthy. I am strong. I am informed. I make sound choices for my family and me. I am responsible, wise, and knowledgeable. I am calm, relaxed, and in Alignment with my decisions and choices. I make choices based on the information I have at the time. I am doing what feels loving for my family and me by providing a safe, healthy environment. Staying home improves my health by decreasing my stress and by not exposing myself to the risk of getting the virus. I'll get more sleep at home, not going out socially.*

7. Can I find the first LES Loop?

More insight can be gained by drawing Awareness to any judgments or criticisms I may have about others, such as, "People are overreacting. People are stupid if they travel. I can't believe they are buying toilet paper." With each projected thought, I have the opportunity to record and reflect on how I may have been overreacting or when I may have overreacted in the past? If I did overreact in the past, how did I feel? How did people react to me when I overreacted? How did I feel when they responded that way? What did I do to try and stop my negative emotions in those instances?

When my ex-husband and a mutual friend came to my house to take my son's bed as part of the settlement after our divorce, I recall trying to stop him from taking the mattress, claiming it was not part of the bed. I know it sounds ludicrous even as I write it on the page, but idiotic behavior often ensues in a triggered moment. I remember our mutual friend giving me that "Really?" look that questioned the stupidity of me trying to keep the mattress separate. I felt embarrassed. I knew it was not logical, it didn't make sense, but I felt the undying need to hold onto that mattress in that moment.

Afterward, I recognized that I really didn't want the mattress. I was trying to hold on to my old life, a time when my family and marriage were intact, and I felt safe. Since I couldn't save the marriage, the least I could do was save the mattress. My brain made the connection that keeping the mattress would help me feel the way I used to feel before the divorce. That, of course, did not happen. Instead, by reacting from a triggered state, I ended up feeling worse than I started by behaving childishly.

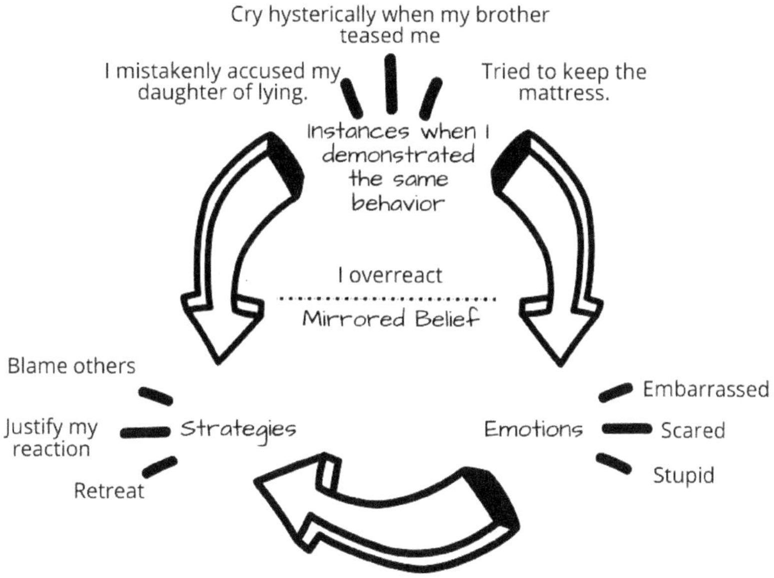

How can I react/behave differently when I feel those emotions the next time they are triggered?

The Alignment Strategy can help draw me back into Alignment where I can perceive the present moment from a space of clarity, where I can observe what is happening outside of me and filter out the facts. It's where I can openly discern between educated recommendations and fear-based suggestions. It's where I can make loving, aligned choices for myself and those around me. Ultimately, it's where we all can move through the consequences of a pandemic and maintain a state of peace, calm, and happiness.

I can also use mirrored beliefs to find the original LES Loop. I took the earliest of the instances noted above in the Loop,

"Crying hysterically when my brother teased me," and used it in the Earliest Memory Loop below.

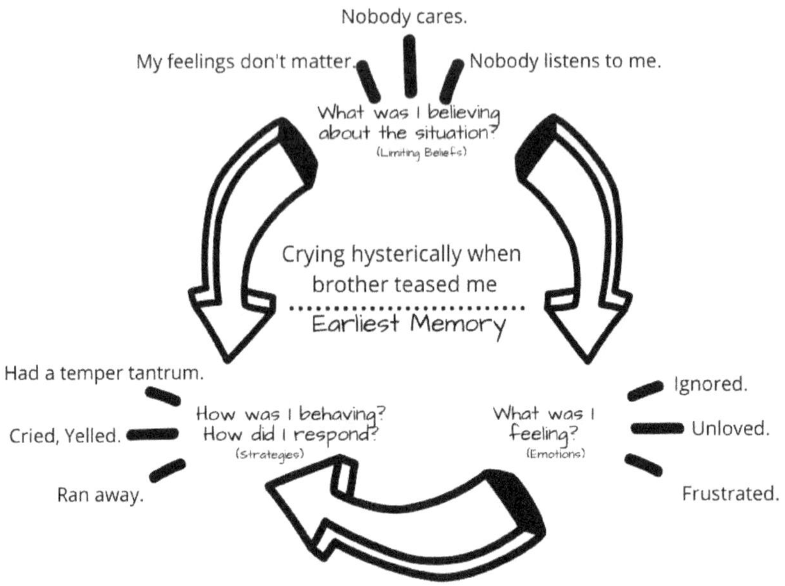

Interestingly, I can see how trying to hold onto the mattress was like an adult temper tantrum. Although my thinking that people were overreacting by buying toilet paper doesn't seem like a big deal, it would have had the power to draw me out of Alignment. Its connection to my early loops (mattress, brother teasing me) could have also moved me far out into the Outside Zone, and that would have made it more difficult for me to move back into Alignment.

8. Question the limiting beliefs from the earliest instance.

Next, I would take each belief from the Earliest Memory Loop (What was I believing about the situation) and ask myself, "Is it true?" I would sit with each thought and contemplate, "Is it true?" knowing that the divine plan was unfolding.

The limiting beliefs originated from the little girl crying hysterically on the floor, not wanting to be teased. No-one stopped the teasing. My perception in that moment created very powerful emotions, and the only way I had to deal with them was to throw a temper tantrum, yell, cry, and run away. Regardless of the behavior of others in that moment, I had alternate perceptions available to me but was too young to consider them. Now, I can open myself up and entertain them. People did care, they listened, and my feelings mattered to them.

Limiting Belief: Nobody cares.

Is that true? No

Alternate possible perceptions of the earliest memory: People care. People did care.

What examples or memories rose up that contradicted my limiting belief?

1. My parents cared. They both worked full time and were probably exhausted.
2. My brother cared. He was probably bored.
3. My brother cared. He may have been teased and was dealing with that by teasing me.

Limiting Belief: Nobody listens to me.

Is that true? No

Alternate possible perceptions of the earliest memory: People listen. People did listen.

What examples or memories rose up that contradicted my limiting belief?

1. My parents listened to me. They signed me up for some activities that I wanted to do.
2. My dog listened to me. He sat when I asked him to sit.
3. My parents listened to me when I was upset about the schoolyard pick and signed me up for the girl's baseball league.

Limiting Belief: My feelings don't matter.

Is that true? No

Alternate possible perceptions of the earliest memory: My feelings do matter. My feelings did matter.

What examples or memories rose up that contradicted my limiting belief?

1. When I ran away, my Dad came looking for me.
2. I remember my Mom sometimes telling my brother to stop it.
3. My Dad helped me deal with some kids that were bullying me.

Even though I had the perception that nobody cared, listened to me, and that my feelings didn't matter, there were alternate perceptions that people did care, listened to me, and respected my feelings that were just as true.

9. Rewrite your story.

I can rewrite my story with a new understanding of myself and how my earliest memory no longer needs to define my experiences.

I care.

I care about myself and my feelings, and I now listen to myself by recognizing the discomfort when I move out of Alignment. I no longer need people outside of me to care, to listen to me because I care and listen to myself. I now take responsibility for my thoughts, my emotions, and my actions. I choose Alignment.

Chapter 9

YOUR CHOICE

By using, "The Alignment Strategy," you will be able to bring Awareness to your thinking, emotions, and behaviors and open up your mind to perceive your situation differently. That openness will help you align your head and heart in the Alignment Zone.

When you find examples of how alternate perceptions can be just as true or truer, you begin to create changes in the way your mind processes the information it receives. Instead of automatically retrieving information from the past, the mind will begin to consider new information, assume that positive perceptions are always available, and make perceiving them, its highest priority.

By completing the LES Loop templates and identifying the instances when the loops were created, you are able to explore your original perceptions and decide if they are still true for you. You get to re-evaluate your strategies and their usefulness. If you begin to acknowledge your emotions, understand what thoughts created them and what behaviors you use to repress them, you can bring conscious choice to how you experience your life. You can choose to live life from the Alignment Zone.

By becoming the author of your experience, you can choose the Alignment Zone as the setting for all future stories to be told.

When you are aligned with Awareness, you are in touch with your greatness. You become open to new ideas, opportunities, and experiences. It's where you can grow, nurture your gifts, and develop different aspects of yourself. It's where synchronicity is like an old friend.

When you live from that aligned place, your greatness oozes up and out of you. You become a tuning fork to the Universe, sensitive to its callings and responsive to its flow. Just when you think it can't get any better, it does.

So, I ask you, would you rather spend your time here on earth, in the perpetual pursuit of satisfying the illusion of lack in the Outside Zone? Or would you rather tap in, and tune in to the greatness you already are? I invite you to expand beyond the mind and explore Awareness and Alignment, so you can live life from your natural state of peace and calm. I invite you to stand in your truth, stay aligned with your true self, and live life from the state of greatness that you already are, in the Alignment Zone.

Chapter 10

THE ALIGNMENT STRATEGY WORKBOOK

In this section, you'll find a guide for the **9 Steps of the Alignment Strategy** to help you identify the Limiting Beliefs, Emotions, Strategies, and Loops that keep you from living life from the Alignment Zone.

9 Steps of the Alignment Strategy

1. When you recognize that you are feeling discomfort or negativity, acknowledge it.
2. Isolate the thought or thoughts you believe to be true.
3. Isolate the strategies you are using to deal with the emotions.
4. Find new, more positive thoughts that embrace an alternate perception.
5. Find examples to support an alternate, more positive thought.
6. Recite a running dialogue of positive self-talk.

7. Find your earliest LES Loop.
8. Question the limiting beliefs from the earliest instance.
9. Rewrite your story.

1. When you recognize that you are feeling discomfort or negativity, acknowledge it.

Draw your awareness to the emotions you're feeling and sensations in your body.

Consider asking yourself,

- Am I annoyed, irritated? Disgusted? Bossy? Pushy?
- Am I angry? Mad? Swearing? Aggressive? Bitter?
- Am I sad, displeased, hurt, depleted, exhausted, unmotivated, disconnected?
- Am I disappointed?
- Do I feel anxious?
- Am I scared? Nervous? Insecure? Nervous? Guarded?
- Am I hurt? Aching? Victimized?
- Am I embarrassed?
- Do I feel rejected? Overlooked?
- Am I feeling powerless? Overwhelmed? Incapable? Weak? Paralyzed?
- Am I feeling small?
- Am I feeling depressed? Self-critical? Lousy? Burdened?
- Am I feeling distrustful? Unsure? Shy? Hesitant?
- Am I feeling numb? Cold? Uncaring?
- Am I lonely? Unhappy?

Physically

- Is my body tense?
- Has my breathing changed? Quickened?
- Am I holding my breath?
- Are my hands clenched?
- Is my jaw tight?
- Does my neck hurt?

- Do I have an upset stomach?
- Does my heart feel empty?
- Are my muscles tense?
- Do I have a furrowed brow?
- Am I getting hot?
- Are my teeth clenched?
- Do I feel sweaty?
- Do I want to vomit?
- Am I trembling?
- Am I stiff?
- Other

---

2. Isolate the thought or thoughts you believe to be true.

There is always a thought that precipitates a negative emotion. The thought is what is triggering the emotion.

Consider asking yourself,

- What am I believing to be true?
- Am I judging the situation or a person?
- Do I want someone to change so I can be happy? What do they need to change?
- Do I want someone to do something different so I won't be upset? What are they doing that is upsetting? If they are doing that, what kind of person does that make them?
- Am I comparing myself to others?
- Am I trying to be right? Pointing out what is wrong?
- Do I want to tell other people what happened? Gossip?

- Am I trying to make myself appear better than someone else?
- Am I trying to make myself appear smaller than someone else?
- Am I trying to control the conversation?
- Am I focused on what should not be happening?

If you can, record your observations below, on your phone, or in a journal.

____

____

3. Isolate the strategies you are using to deal with the emotions.

What actions do I take, or what behaviors do I engage in to repress or deal with the negative emotions?

____

____

Have I had this type of experience before? If so, what was the experience?

____

____

Have I responded like this in the past? If so, what proceeded the response?

What do I believe would happen if I no longer responded that way?

What do I hope to achieve by acting this way?

What experience am I trying to prevent from happening? If I couldn't prevent it from happening, describe the potential impact.

4. Find new, more positive thoughts that embrace an alternate perception.

Insert one of the negative thoughts you were thinking in a thought bubble below. Next, find alternative, more positive thoughts to help move back into alignment.

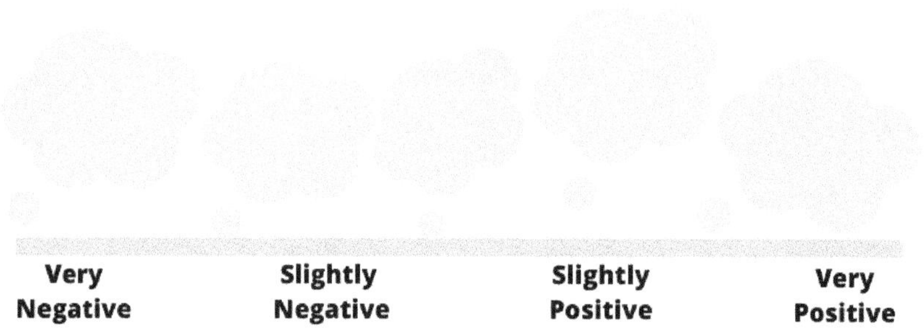

5. Find examples to support an alternate, more positive thought.

Once you have entertained alternate, more positive perceptions, it is important to find real examples of how those new perceptions could be just as true or truer. Finding proof helps to anchor the new perception in your brain and gives it emotional power to counterbalance the negative thought and the negatively charged evidence attached to the negative thoughts. Choose 3 of the more positive thoughts from #4 and find evidence for each.

Example:

Limiting Belief – I can't go to work like this.

Alternate perception - I can go to work like this.

Evidence

- *I've spilled on my shirt at work before.*
- *What my shirt looks like has nothing to do with me being able to go to work.*
- *The stain on my shirt does not prevent me from driving.*

Limiting Belief - ______________________________
Alternate perception - __________________________
Evidence

1. ______________________________
2. ______________________________
3. ______________________________

Limiting Belief - ______________________________
Alternate perception - __________________________
Evidence

1. ______________________________
2. ______________________________
3. ______________________________

Limiting Belief - ______________________________
Alternate perception - __________________________
Evidence

1. ______________________________
2. ______________________________
3. ______________________________

6. Recite a running dialogue of positive self-talk

Get your brain to consider:

- What am I gaining?
- How is this for me?
- What gifts am I receiving?

Next, use your answers to those questions, and all of the alternate positive perceptions and evidential support you found in #5 above, to create a running dialogue or mantra.

____

____

____

____

____

7. Find your Earliest LES Loop

There are two templates to help you discover the original LES Loop.

A) Limiting Belief "I" Statement Template. This template is for situations when you have a simple belief about yourself.

> *Example: I am not worthy. I am not enough. I am too much. I am not smart. I am a failure. I am a disappointment.*

B) Mirroring Template. This template is used when our limiting beliefs or projections are focused on a situation, person, behavior, a want, or a need, and the "I" Statement is not obvious. *Example: He is late. George is late. She is stupid. Ben is ig-*

noring me. He doesn't love me. It doesn't matter. My meal was cold. My car broke down. My car was stuck. My bills are overdue.

A). "I" STATEMENT LES TEMPLATE

Use this template for **Limiting Belief "I" Statements** that are straightforward and obvious, such as, "I am lonely. I am not worthy. I am fat. I am lazy."

1. Record the **Limiting Belief "I" Statement** in the middle of the LES Loop on the dotted line.
2. Complete the LES Loop below by recording the Limiting Beliefs, Emotions, and Strategies triggered by the "I" Statement.

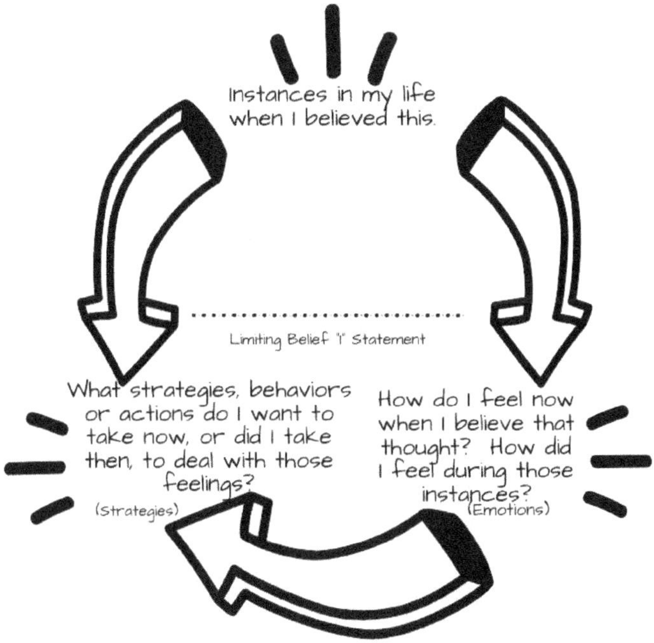

3. Choose the earliest instance from the LES Loop above and record it in the LES Loop center below.

For example, a memory at age 6 is earlier than a memory at age 20. Be aware that sometimes, you may complete the above loop, and other memories might surface as well. Find the earliest memory whenever possible, whether it was one of the three recorded in the loop or a passing memory that was not recorded. Try to work with the earliest memory or the memory with the biggest negative, emotional charge.

4. Complete the loop below by recording your Limiting Beliefs, Emotions, and Strategies experienced during that earliest memory.

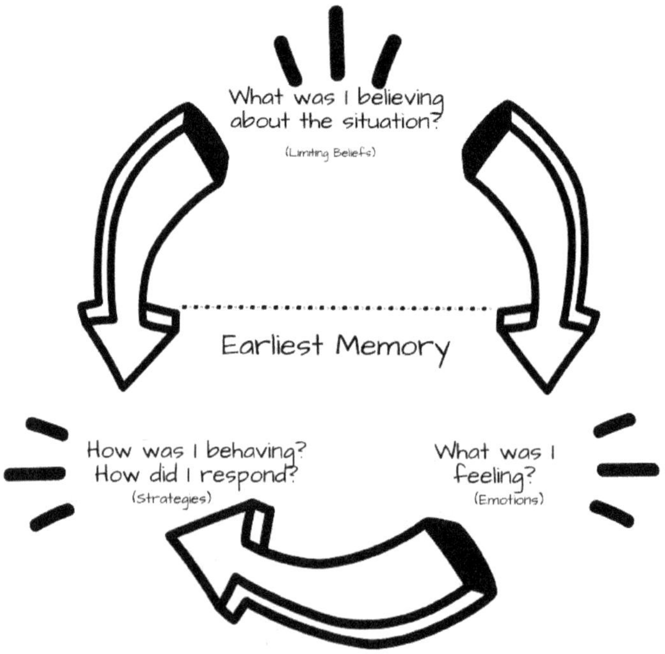

B) MIRRORED BELIEF LES TEMPLATE

This template is used when your limiting beliefs and projections are focused on a situation, person, behavior, a want, or a need, and the "I" Statement is not clear. Record what the situation was in the middle of the LES Loop on the dotted line.

Example: Present situation could be that George is late, someone butted in line, the neighbor pulled the stake out of the ground.

1. Complete the LES Loop by recording the Limiting Beliefs, Emotions, and Strategies triggered by the situation.

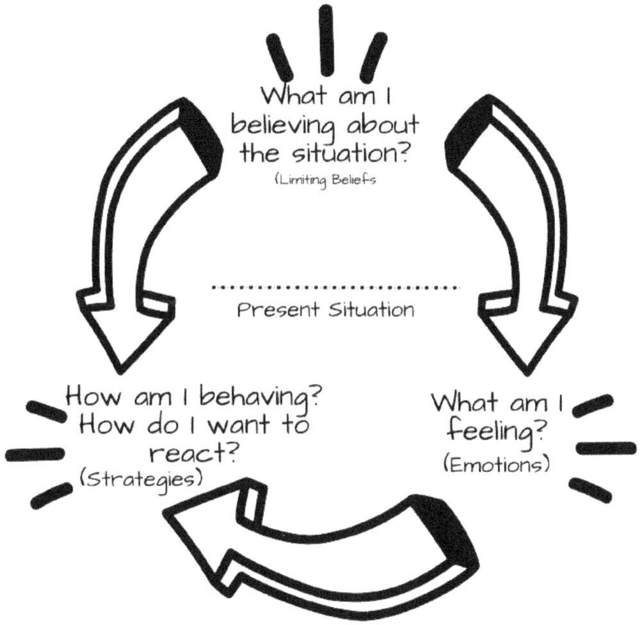

2. Identifying the "I" Statement.

In the above loop, you identified limiting beliefs that you believed about the present situation. Choose the limiting belief that has the biggest negative charge or the one that jumps out at you and create an "I" statement. Return to **Finding the "I" Statement** in Chapter 6 for assistance if necessary.

Example: If the Limiting Belief was, "He was ignoring me," the "I" Statement would be, "I am ignoring me."
If the Limiting Belief was, "They are killing the planet," the "I" Statement would be, "I am killing me.

3. Record the "I" Statement in the center of the LES Loop below.

4. Complete the LES Loop below by recording the instances in your life when you believed the "I" Statement to be true, the emotions you had during those instances, and the strategies you used to deal with the emotions.

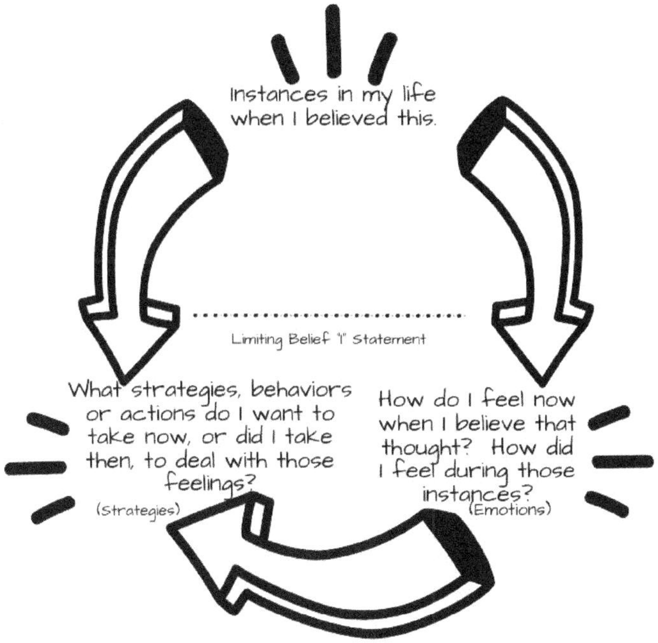

5. Choose the earliest instance from the LES Loop above and record it in the LES Loop center below. For example, a memory at age 6 is earlier than a memory at age 20. Be aware that sometimes, you may complete the above loop, and other memories might surface as well. Find the earliest memory whenever possible, whether it was one of the three recorded in the loop or a passing memory that was not recorded. Try to work with the earliest memory or the memory with the biggest negative, emotional charge.

6. Complete the loop below by recording your Limiting Beliefs, Emotions, and Strategies experienced during that earliest memory.

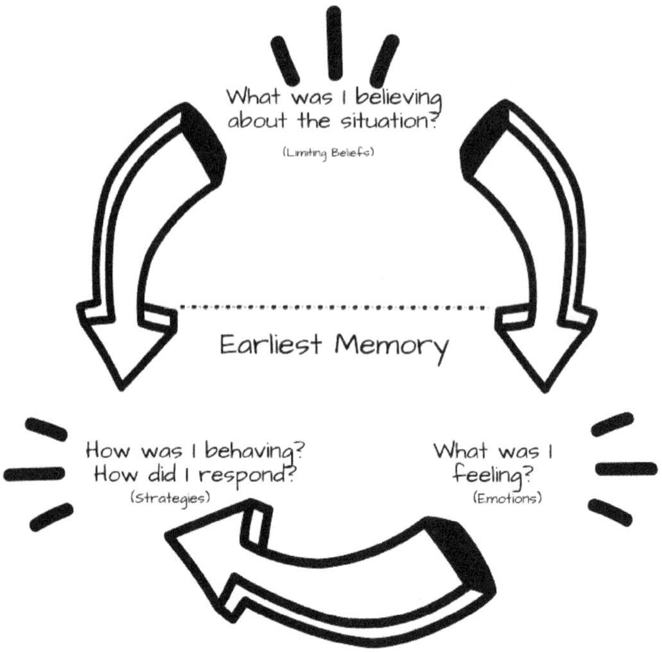

8. Question the limiting beliefs from the earliest instance.

Take each belief from the Earliest Memory Loop (What did I believe about the situation?), and ask yourself, "Is it true?" Sit with the thought while in alignment, knowing that you are the divine plan unfolding.

Example:
Limiting Belief: *I am alone.*
Is that true? *No*
Alternate possible perceptions of the earliest memory: *I am not alone. I was not alone.*
What examples rose up that contradicted my limiting belief?

What memories rose up within me where I was not alone? What other perceptions came to light that indicated I was not alone?

1. *I was surrounded by adults.*
2. *My friend's parents wanted to adopt me.*
3. *My friend's parents took me on vacation with them.*

Limiting Belief: ______________________________

Is that true? _____
Alternate possible perceptions of the earliest memory:
What examples or memories rose up that contradicted my limiting belief?

1. ____

2. ____

3. ____

Limiting Belief: ______________________________

Is that true? _____
Alternate possible perceptions of the earliest memory:
What examples or memories rose up that contradicted my limiting belief?

1. ____

2. ____

3. ____

Limiting Belief: ______________________

Is that true? _____

Alternate possible perceptions of the earliest memory:

What examples or memories rose up that contradicted my limiting belief?

1. ______________________________________

2. ______________________________________

3. ______________________________________

9. Rewrite your story.

A. Rewrite the story with a new understanding of how the earliest experience can be perceived differently using your new, positive thoughts and perceptions.

____

____

____

____

B. Rewrite the programmed responses. How will you respond if the old loop gets triggered again? What new strategies can you engage in based on your new story and understanding?

Complete the following:

When I feel __________________, __________________, and

______________________ *(Insert emotions from old, earliest*

instance loop) my habitual way of dealing with those

emotions is to _________________________________,

____,

and ____.
(Insert strategies from earliest memory LES loop).

I now choose to

____,

____, or

____instead.
(Insert new strategies of how you wish to respond if the loop is triggered again)

EMOTIONS LIST

Emotions List

Often our emotions are bundled together by a simple, non-descriptive word such as sad or mad. This list of emotions can help you complete the LES Loops and give a voice to the variety of feelings you may have buried. This makes it easier to see patterns and connections as well.

Angry	Hurt	Distressed	Scared	Sad
Irate	aching	harassed	afraid	depressed
annoyed	aggrieved	peeved	anxious	devastated
cross	agonized	agitated	fearful	unhappy
vexed	battered	anxious	panicked	lonely
irritated	bleeding	distraught	startled	unworthy
exasperated	bruised	jittery	petrified	crying
provoked	burned	perturbed	shaken	moaning
testy	damaged	shaky	terrified	empty
mad	offended	bothered	frozen	desperate
crabby	pained	bugged	alarmed	moody
seething	scarred	concerned	dreading	self-depreciating
infuriated	tortured	spooked	wary	stuck
displeased	sad	worried	cowardly	tired
raging	unhappy	bummed out	suspicious	exhausted
livid	distant	bundle of nerves	nervous	low

pissed	slighted	fidgety	frightened	bummed out
enraged	smothered	jumpy	disturbed	crummy
offended	bullied	shook up	rattled	cheerless
hateful	slighted	uptight	spooked	negative
fuming	belittled	helpless	worried	dissatisfied
huffy	sad	paralyzed	troubled	down
outraged	insulted	overwhelmed	guarded	resistant
hot	upset	Shut down	paranoid	lost
resentful	provoked	inferior	unwelcoming	self-loathing
mean	dejected	vulnerable	uptight	directionless
violent	downcast	trapped	attacking	bitter
yelling	crushed	weak	immobile	heartbroken
bitter	confused	incompetent	timid	gloomy
revengeful	wronged	useless	overpowered	blue
retaliating		paralyzed		troubled
attacked		uncertain		cold
ranting		uneasy		lifeless
serious		stressed		numb
bossy		hesitant		bored
arrogant		distracted		uninterested
superior		conflicted		dull
faultfinding				crabby
glaring				miserable
unfair				alienated
scolding				contracted
demanding				touchy
rude				no energy

CPSIA information can be obtained
at www.ICGtesting.com
Printed in the USA
BVHW042012180221
600536BV00006B/19

9 781777 153700